AMERICAN LEAGUE

THE OFFICIAL
MAJOR LEAGUE BASEBALL

MAJOR LEAGUE BASEBALL®

SEASON GUIDE
1993

CADER BOOKS

W.W. NORTON & COMPANY

New York   London

© 1993 Major League Baseball Properties, Inc.
All rights reserved.
Reproduction in whole or in part without permission is prohibited.
The Major League Club insignias depicted in this product are the exclusive property of the respective Major League Clubs and may not be reproduced without their written consent.
Printed in the United States of America.

1992 rosters and individual statistics provided by the Major League Baseball-IBM information system.

Produced by Cader Books.
Cover design: Michael Cader

The text of this book is comsped in 6/8 Helvetica
with display set in 14 point Copperplate.

ISBN 0-393-31045-0 (paper)
ISBN 0-393-31050-7 (paper: 20-copy pre-pack)

W. W. Norton & Company, Inc.
500 Fifth Avenue
New York, NY 10110
W. W. Norton & Company Ltd.,
10 Coptic Street, London WC1A 1PU

1 2 3 4 5 6 7 8 9 10

CONTENTS

Spring Training Schedule	4
Nationally Televised Games	7
1992 Final Standings	8
All-Star Game Results	9
League Championship Series Results	11
World Series Results	12
Awards	14
1993 Milestones	15
1992 Minor League Results (AAA and AA)	18
1992 Individual Leaders	20
Team-by-Team Records, 1992 Rosters, and	23
Contact & Ticket Information:	
Baltimore Orioles (Bal)	23
Boston Red Sox (Bos)	26
California Angels (Cal)	29
Chicago White Sox (CWS)	32
Cleveland Indians (Cle)	35
Detroit Tigers (Det)	38
Kansas City Royals (KC)	41
Milwaukee Brewers (Mil)	44
Minnesota Twins (Min)	47
New York Yankees (NYY)	50
Oakland Athletics (Oak)	53
Seattle Mariners (Sea)	56
Texas Rangers (Tex)	59
Toronto Blue Jays (Tor)	62

SPRING TRAINING SCHEDULE

KEY
+ Night game
* Split squad

• Home teams are listed second.
• Clubs play at home except where otherwise noted.
• This schedule is subject to change.
• Home locations are as follows:

Atl: W. Palm Beach
Bal: St. Petersburg
Bos: Lee County
Chi: Mesa
CWS: Sarasota
Cin: Plant City
Cle: Homestead
Col: Tuscon
Det: Lakeland
Fla: Cocoa
KC: Baseball City
LA: Vero Beach
Mil: Chandler
Min: Ft. Myers
NYM: Port St.Lucie
NYY: Ft. Lauderdale
Oak: Phoenix
Phi: Clearwater
Pit: Bradenton
StL: St. Petersburg
SD: Yuma
SF: Scottsdale
Tex: Port Charlotte
Tor: Dunedin

March 4
Ga. Tech vs. Atl
Pit vs. CWS
Central Florida U. vs. KC
Edison College vs. Min+

March 5
Hou vs. Fla
Min vs. Cin
NYY vs. LA
Bal vs. Pit
NYM vs. KC
CWS vs. Det
Tor vs. Tex
SF vs. Chi
Cal vs. SD
Oak vs. Mil

March 6
Mon vs. Atl
LA vs. Hou
Cin vs. Pit
Tor vs. Phi
Bal vs. StL
Fla vs. Cle
NYM vs. NYY
Min vs. Bos
KC vs. Det
CWS vs. Tex
SF vs. Col
Cal vs. SD
Chi vs. Mil
Sea vs. Oak

March 7
Phi vs. Cin
Atl vs. Mon
NYY vs. NYM
Tex vs. Pit
StL vs. Bal
Fla vs. Cle
Det vs. KC
Bos vs. Min
CWS vs. Tor
SF vs. Chi
Col vs. SD
Oak vs. Cal
Sea vs. Mil

March 8
LA vs. Fla
Atl vs. NYM
Phi vs. Pit
Det vs. Cin
NYY vs. Mon
Tor vs. StL
Hou vs. Cle
Min* vs. CWS
Tex* vs. Bos
Bal vs. KC
Tex* vs. Min*
Col vs. SD
SF vs. Mil
Chi vs. Oak
Sea vs. Cal

March 9
NYM vs. Atl
Fla* vs. LA
Cin vs. StL
Hou* vs. Fla*
KC vs. Hou*
Bal vs. Phi
Pit vs. Bos
Mon vs. NYY
CWS vs. Cle*+
Tor* vs. Det
Min vs. Tex
Cle* vs. Tor*
Cal* vs. Col*
Oak vs. SD+
Col* vs. Cal*
Sea vs. Mil

March 10
Hou vs. Cin
Mon vs. NYM
NYY vs. Atl
KC vs. LA
Pit vs. Bal+
StL vs. Tex
Phi vs. Tor
Bos vs. Min
CWS vs. Cle
Cal vs. Chi
Mil vs. Col
Oak* vs. SD

Sea vs. SF*
SF* vs. Oak*

March 11
Fla vs. Cin
Atl vs. LA
NYM vs. Mon
StL vs. Phi
Min vs. Pit
Hou vs. Det
Tor vs. Bal+
Tex vs. Bos
Cle vs. KC
CWS vs. NYY
Chi vs. Col
SF vs. Cal
SD vs. Mil
Sea vs. Oak

March 12
NYM vs. Hou
LA vs. Mon+
Pit vs. Phi
NYY* vs. Atl*
Cle vs. Fla
Bos* vs. StL
Cin vs. Tor*
Atl* vs. Bos*
Bal vs. CWS*
Tor* vs. Cle*
Det vs. KC
Tex vs. Min
CWS* vs. NYY*
SD vs. Chi
Col* vs. SF
Sea* vs. Col*
Sea* vs. Cal
Mil vs. Oak

March 13
Mon vs. Atl
Phi vs. Cin
Fla vs. NYM
Pit vs. StL
Det vs. Hou*
Hou* vs. KC*
LA vs. NYY
Bos vs. CWS
KC* vs. Cle
Tor vs. Min
Bal vs. Tex

SPRING TRAINING SCHEDULE

Col vs. Chi	SD vs. Chi	Col vs. Oak+	Det* vs. CWS*
Oak vs. SF	Oak vs. Col	Sea vs. Cal	CWS* vs. Tex
SD vs. Cal	Sea vs. Cal	**March 20**	SF vs. Col
Sea vs. Mil	**March 17**	NYM* vs. Atl	SD vs. Mil
March 14	Atl vs. Hou	StL vs. Cin	Chi vs. Bos
Atl vs. Fla	Phi vs. LA	Mon* vs. Fla	Sea vs. Cal
NYM vs. LA	NYM vs. Mon	Mon* vs. LA*	**March 23**
NYY vs. Mon	Fla vs. Pit	Det vs. Hou	Fla vs. Mon
Min vs. Phi	KC vs. Cin	KC* vs. NYM*	Hou vs. NYM
Tor vs. Pit	Tex* vs. StL	Pit vs. Bal	Cin vs. Phi+
Cin vs. Bal	NYY* vs. Bos	Phi vs. KC*	Tex vs. Pit
Hou vs. Det	Tor vs. CWS	Min* vs. Cle	Tor vs. StL+
StL vs. KC	Bal vs. Det	Bos* vs. Min*	LA vs. KC
Tex vs. Bos	Cle vs. Mon	Bos* vs. NYY	Bal vs. Cle
Cle vs. CWS	NYY* vs. Tex*+	CWS vs. Tex	Bos vs. Det
SD vs. SF	SD vs. Col	LA* vs. Tor Toronto	Oak vs. Chi
Sea vs. Chi	Chi vs. SF	SD vs. Col	Mil vs. SF
Cal vs. Col	Sea vs. Mil	Chi vs. SF	Col vs. Cal
Mil vs. Oak	**March 18**	Mil vs. Cal	**March 24**
March 15	Mon vs. Atl	Sea vs. Oak	Fla vs. Hou+
Mon vs. Atl	Hou vs. Fla	**March 21**	Atl vs. LA
NYM vs. Fla	LA vs. NYM	Hou vs. Cin	NYY vs. Mon
LA vs. Hou	StL vs. Pit	Fla vs. LA	Det vs. Phi
Cin vs. StL	Det vs. Cin	Atl vs. Mon	Cin vs. Bal
CWS vs. Pit	KC vs. Phi	Phi vs. StL	NYM vs. Cle
Phi vs. NYY	Min vs. Bal	Cle* vs. NYM	Pit vs. Tor
Det vs. Bos	NYY vs. CWS	Pit vs. Min	CWS vs. Min+
Bal vs. Min	Bos vs. Cle	CWS vs. Bos	Bos vs. Tex
Cle vs. Tex	Tex vs. Tor	Cle* vs. KC*	SF vs. SD+
KC vs. Tor	Oak vs. Chi	KC* vs. Det	Mil vs. Chi
Mil* vs. Col*	Sea vs. SF+	Bal vs. NYY	Cal vs. Col
Sea vs. SF	Col vs. Cal+	Tex vs. Tor	Sea vs. Oak
Chi vs. Cal	SD vs. Mil	Sea vs. Chi	**March 25**
Col* vs. Mil*	**March 19**	Mil* vs. Col*	NYM vs. Fla
SD vs. Oak	Atl vs. Fla	Oak* vs. SF*	Hou vs. LA
March 16	NYM vs. Mon	SD vs. Cal	Tor vs. Cin
Cin vs. Hou	Pit vs. StL	Col* vs. Mil*	StL vs. Bos
LA vs. Mon	Bal vs. Phi	SF* vs. Oak*	Pit vs. CWS+
Phi vs. NYM+	Cin vs. Det	**March 22**	Atl vs. NYY
Det vs. Fla*	Hou vs. KC	Fla vs. Atl*	Bal vs. Cle
Fla* vs. CWS*	LA* vs. NYY*	Mon vs. NYM	Det vs. KC
Atl vs. KC*	NYY* vs. CWS	NYY* vs. LA	Min vs. Tex
Pit vs. Tex	Bos vs. Cle	KC vs. StL	Chi vs. Col
StL vs. Tor	Tex vs. Min	Cin vs. Det*+	SF vs. SD
CWS* vs. Bal+	LA vs. Tor+ Toronto	Atl* vs. NYY	Sea vs. Mil
Cle* vs. Bos+		Phi vs. Tor+	Cal vs. Oak
KC* vs. Cle*	SD vs. SF	Min vs. Bos	**March 26**
NYY vs. Min	Chi vs. Mil		LA vs. Atl

5

SPRING TRAINING SCHEDULE

Phi	vs.	Pit				Cle	vs.	Fla
KC	vs.	Cin				Min	vs.	Phi
Mon	vs.	NYY				CWS	vs.	Pit
Fla	vs.	Cle				StL	vs.	Det
StL	vs.	Det				Cin	vs.	KC+
Tex	vs.	Bal				Mon	vs.	NYY
Bos	vs.	CWS				Bos	vs.	Tex
Min	vs.	Tor				Bal	vs.	Tor
NYM*	vs.	Oak*+				Col	vs.	Chi
	New Orleans					Sea	vs.	Mil
Oak*	vs.	Chi				**April 2**		
Sea	vs.	Col+				Atl	vs.	Mon
Mil	vs.	SD+				Det	vs.	Cin
Cal	vs.	SF+				Bos	vs.	Phi
March 27						StL	vs.	Tor
Fla	vs.	Mon				Portland vs. Min		
LA	vs.	NYM*				Col	vs.	Col
NYY	vs.	Atl+					Springs Sky	
Tor	vs.	Phi					Sox (Tucson)	
Cle	vs.	Pit				KC	vs.	Fla+
StL	vs.	Bal					Jacksonville	
Cin	vs.	Det				Tex	vs.	Hou+
Hou	vs.	KC+					Houston	
Tex	vs.	CWS				Cal	vs.	LA +
Bos	vs.	Min					Los Angeles	
NYM*	vs.	Oak*+				CWS	vs.	SD+
	New Orleans						Las Vegas	
SF	vs.	Chi				NYY	vs.	NYM
Sea	vs.	Col					Washington, D.C.	
Mil	vs.	SD				Pit	vs.	Bal
Oak*	vs.	Cal+					Baltimore	
March 28						SF	vs.	Oak+
NYM	vs.	Atl					Oakland	
Mon	vs.	LA				Mil	vs.	Sea
Phi	vs.	StL					Las Vegas	
NYY	vs.	Fla				**April 3**		
KC	vs.	Hou				Phi	vs.	StL
Pit	vs.	CWS				Mon	vs.	LA*
Cin	vs.	Cle				Phi	vs.	StL
Min	vs.	Bos					Ok. City	
Bal	vs.	Tex				Bos	vs.	Atl
Det	vs.	Tor					Atlanta	
Cal*	vs.	Col*				Cle	vs.	Cin
Sea	vs.	SD					Columbus	
Cal*	vs.	SF				NYY	vs.	NYM
Chi	vs.	Oak+					NY/Shea	
Col*	vs.	Mil				Fla	vs.	KC
							Jacksonville	

March 29
LA	vs.	Atl
Mon	vs.	NYM
StL	vs.	Phi
Det	vs.	Cin+
Cle	vs.	Hou
Bos	vs.	Pit
Fla	vs.	NYY
Tex	vs.	Bal
Min	vs.	CWS+
Tor	vs.	KC
SF	vs.	Col
Cal	vs.	Chi
Sea	vs.	SD
Oak	vs.	Mil

March 30
Fla	vs.	Mon
LA	vs.	NYM
StL	vs.	Pit
KC	vs.	Hou
Tor	vs.	Phi
Cin	vs.	Cle
Atl	vs.	NYY
Det	vs.	Bal+
Min	vs.	Bos
Tex	vs.	CWS+
SF	vs.	Chi
Sea	vs.	SD
Col	vs.	Oak
Cal	vs.	Mil

March 31
Mon	vs.	Fla
NYM	vs.	LA
NYY	vs.	Atl
Tor	vs.	Cin
Cle	vs.	Hou
Bal	vs.	StL
Phi	vs.	Min
Pit	vs.	Tex+
CWS	vs.	Bos
KC	vs.	Det
Chi	vs.	SD
Col	vs.	SF
Mil	vs.	Cal
Sea	vs.	Oak

April 1
LA*	vs.	Atl
Hou	vs.	NYM

Hou	vs.	Tex
	Arlington	
LA*	vs.	Cal+
	Anaheim	
Chi	vs.	CWS
	Las Vegas	
SD	vs.	Las
	Vegas Stars+	
	Las Vegas	
Pit	vs.	Bal
	Washington, D.C.	
Col	vs.	Min
	Minneapolis	
SF	vs.	Oak
	Oakland	
Mil	vs.	Sea
	Vancouver	
Det	vs.	Tor+
	Vancouver	

April 4
LA	vs.	Mon
Phi	vs.	StL
	Ok. City	
Oak	vs.	SF
	San Francisco	
SD	vs.	Cal
	Anaheim	
Col	vs.	Min
	Minneapolis	
NYM	vs.	NYY
	NY/Yankee	
Det	vs.	Sea
	Vancouver	
Mil	vs.	Tor+
	Vancouver	

NATIONALLY TELEVISED GAMES

CBS

Day	Teams			Time (ET)
Apr. 17	NYM	vs.	Cin	1:00 PM
	Chi	vs.	Bos	
Apr. 24	Cin	vs.	Chi	1:00 PM
	Fla	vs.	Col	11:15 AM (MT)
May 1	StL	vs.	Atl	1:00 PM
	Min	vs.	Det	
	Mil	vs.	Tex	
May 8	Bal	vs.	Tor	1:00 Nat
May 15	LA	vs.	Hou	1:00 PM
	NYM	vs.	Mon	
	Bos	vs.	Min	
May 22	Oak	vs.	Chi	1:00 PM
	Atl	vs.	NYM	
	Cal	vs.	Tex	
May 29	Mon	vs.	CWS	1:00 PM
	LA	vs.	Pit	
	SD	vs.	StL	
July 10	CWS	vs.	Bal	3:00 PM
	Cin	vs.	Pit	
	NYY	vs.	Cal	
July 17	Oak	vs.	NYY	1:00 PM
	Hou	vs.	StL	
	KC	vs.	Tor	
July 24	NYM	vs.	LA	3:00 PM
	Chi	vs.	Hou	
	Bal	vs.	Min	
July 31	Atl	vs.	Hou	1:00 PM
	Det	vs.	Tor	
	SD	vs.	Cin	
Aug. 7	Chi	vs.	StL	1:00 PM
	Bos	vs.	Det	
	Pit	vs.	NYM	
Aug. 28	Chi	vs.	Atl	1:00 PM
	Bos	vs.	KC	
	Cal	vs.	Mil	
Sept. 18	To be announced*			
Sept. 25	To be announced*			
Oct. 2	To be announced*			

*First pitch will be between 2:00 and 3:00 PM ET.

ESPN

Day	Teams			First Pitch (ET)
Apr. 5	LA	vs.	Fla	2:05 PM
	Mon	vs.	Cin*	
	Phi	vs.	Hou	7:35 PM
	Col	vs.	NY*	(taped from 2:05)
Apr. 11	Cin	vs.	StL	8:05 PM
Apr. 18	Pit	vs.	LA	8:05 PM
Apr. 25	Bos	vs.	Cal	8:05 PM
May 2	Col	vs.	Fla	8:05 PM
May 9	Cin	vs.	Hou	8:05 PM
May 16	SF	vs.	SD	8:05 PM
May 23	NYY	vs.	Bos	8:05 PM
	Sea	vs.	KC*	
May 30	Det	vs.	Sea	8:05 PM
May 31	NYM	vs.	Chi	4:05 PM
	Tor	vs.	Cal*	
	Phi	vs.	Cin	7:35 PM
	SD	vs.	Atl*	
June 6	Chi	vs.	Mon	8:05 PM
	NYY	vs.	Tex*	
June 13	NYY	vs.	Mil	8:05 PM
	Cle	vs.	Tex*	
June 20	NYM	vs.	Pit	8:05 PM
June 27	KC	vs.	Cle	8:05 PM
	Oak	vs.	Tex*	
July 4	SD	vs.	Phi	8:05 PM
	Bos	vs.	Sea*	
July 5	Pit	vs.	Cin	2:05 PM
	Tex	vs.	Mil*	
	CWS	vs.	Tor	7:35 PM
	SD	vs.	NYM*	
July 11	LA	vs.	NYM	8:05 PM
July 18	Oak	vs.	NYY	8:05 PM
	Det	vs.	Tex*	
July 25	Tor	vs.	Tex	8:05 PM
Aug. 1	Tex	vs.	Oak	8:05 PM
	Chi	vs.	Sea*	
Aug. 8	Mil	vs.	Tor	8:05 PM
	Sea	vs.	Tex*	
Aug 15	Atl	vs.	Cin	8:05 PM
Aug. 22	Atl	vs.	Cin	8:05 PM
Aug. 29	Min	vs.	CWS	8:05 PM
Sept. 5	Tex	vs.	Min	8:05 PM
Sept. 12	Oak	vs.	Bal	8:05 PM
Sept. 19	NYM	vs.	Atl	8:05 PM

* Back-up game

1992 FINAL STANDINGS

EASTERN DIVISION

Team	W	L	PCT.	GB
TORONTO	96	66	.593	-
MILWAUKEE	92	70	.568	4.0
BALTIMORE	89	73	.549	7.0
NEW YORK	76	86	.469	20.0
CLEVELAND	76	86	.469	20.0
DETROIT	75	87	.463	21.0
BOSTON	73	89	.451	23.0

Victories Vs. Eastern Division Teams

Team	TOR	MIL	BAL	NY	CLE	DET	BOS	Vs. EAST
TORONTO	-	5	8	11	7	8	6	45
MILWAUKEE	8	-	7	6	8	8	8	45
BALTIMORE	5	6	-	5	7	10	8	41
NEW YORK	2	7	8	-	6	8	6	37
CLEVELAND	6	5	6	7	-	5	7	36
DETROIT	5	5	3	5	8	-	9	35
BOSTON	7	5	5	7	6	4	-	34
TOTALS	33	33	37	41	42	43	44	273

WESTERN DIVISION

Team	W	L	PCT.	GB
OAKLAND	96	66	.593	-
MINNESOTA	90	72	.556	6.0
CHICAGO	86	76	.531	10.0
TEXAS	77	85	.475	19.0
KANSAS CITY	72	90	.444	24.0
CALIFORNIA	72	90	.444	24.0
SEATTLE	64	98	.395	32.0

Victories Vs. Western Division Teams

Team	OAK	MIN	CWS	TEX	KC	CAL	SEA	Vs. WEST
OAKLAND	-	8	8	9	9	8	12	54
MINNESOTA	5	-	5	6	7	11	8	42
CHICAGO	5	8	-	5	7	10	4	39
TEXAS	4	7	8	-	7	4	9	39
KANSAS CITY	4	6	6	6	-	5	7	34
CALIFORNIA	5	2	3	9	8	-	7	34
SEATTLE	1	5	9	4	6	6	-	31
TOTALS	24	36	39	39	44	44	47	273

ALL-STAR GAME

Year	Date	Winner	Score	Year	Date	Winner	Score
1933	July 6	American	4-2	1969	July 23	National	9-3
1934	July 10	American	9-7	1970	July 14	National	5-4
1935	July 8	American	4-1	1971	July 13	American	6-4
1936	July 7	National	4-3	1972	July 25	National	4-3
1937	July 7	American	8-3	1973	July 24	National	7-1
1938	July 6	National	4-1	1974	July 23	National	7-2
1939	July 11	American	3-1	1975	July 15	National	6-3
1940	July 9	National	4-0	1976	July 13	National	7-1
1941	July 8	American	7-5	1977	July 19	National	7-5
1942	July 6	American	3-1	1978	July 11	National	7-3
1943	July 13	American	5-3	1979	July 17	National	7-6
1944	July11	National	7-1	1980	July 8	National	4-2
1945	No game due to wartime travel restrictions			1981	August 9	National	5-4
				1982	July 13	National	4-1
1946	July 9	American	12-0	1983	July 6	American	13-3
1947	July 8	American	2-1	1984	July 10	National	3-1
1948	July 13	American	5-2	1985	July 16	National	6-1
1949	July 12	American	11-7	1986	July 15	American	3-2
1950	July 11	National	4-3	1987	July 14	National	2-0
1951	July 10	National	8-3	1988	July 12	American	2-1
1952	July 8	National	3-2	1989	July 11	American	5-3
1953	July 14	National	5-1	1990	July 10	American	2-0
1954	July 13	American	11-9	1991	July 9	American	4-2
1955	July 12	National	6-5	1992	July 14	American	13-6
1956	July 10	National	7-3				
1957	July 9	American	6-5				
1958	July 8	American	4-3				
1959	July 7	National	5-4				
	August 3	American	5-3				
1960	July 11	National	5-3				
	July 13	National	6-0				
1961	July11	National	5-4				
	July 31	Tie*	1-1				
1962	July 10	National	3-1				
	July 30	American	9-4				
1963	July 9	National	5-3				
1964	July 7	National	7-4				
1965	July 13	National	6-5				
1966	July 12	National	2-1				
1967	July 11	National	2-1				
1968	July 9	National	1-0				

*Game called because of rain after nine innings

ALL-STAR GAME

Most Valuable Player

Year	Player/Team	Pos.
1962 (1)	Maury Wills, LA (NL)	SS
(2)	Leon Wagner, LA (AL)	LF
1963	Willie Mays, SF	CF
1964	Johnny Callison, Phil	RF
1965	Juan Marichal, SF	P
1966	Brooks Robinson, Bal	3B
1967	Tony Perez, Cin	3B
1968	Willie Mays, SF	CF
1969	Willie McCovey, SF	1B
1970	Carl Yastrzemski, Bos	CF
1971	Frank Robinson, Bal	RF
1972	Joe Morgan, Cin	2B
1973	Bobby Bonds, SF	RF
1974	Steve Garvey, LA	1B
1975	Bill Madlock, Chi (NL)	3B
	Jon Matlack, NY (NL)	P
1976	George Foster, Cin	CF-RF
1977	Don Sutton, LA	P
1978	Steve Garvey, LA	1B
1979	Dave Parker, Pitt	RF
1980	Ken Griffey, Cin	LF
1981	Gary Carter, Mon	C
1982	Dave Concepcion, Cin	SS
1983	Fred Lynn, Cal	CF
1984	Gary Carter, Mon	C
1985	LaMarr Hoyt, SD	P
1986	Roger Clemens, Bos	P
1987	Tim Raines, Mon	LF
1988	Terry Steinbach, Oak	C
1989	Bo Jackson, KC	LF
1990	Julio Franco, Tex	2B
1991	Cal Ripken, Balt.	SS
1992	Ken Griffey Jr., Sea	CF

All-Time Top Vote-Getters

Player	Total Votes
Rod Carew	32,366,682
George Brett	27,251,788
Mike Schmidt	26,199,385
Carlton Fisk	24,529,941
Steve Garvey	22,694,088
Pete Rose	22,617,715
Johnny Bench	22,436,134
Reggie Jackson	22,292,563
Ozzie Smith	20,643,394
Fred Lynn	19,637,800
Dave Concepcion	19,523,657
Joe Morgan	18,024,443

1992 Linescore

American League   4 1 1   0 0 4   0 3 0 — 13 19 1
National League   0 0 0   0 0 1   0 3 2 — 6 12 1

E—Molitor, Kruk. **DP**—AL 1. **LOB:** American League 6, National League 7.
2B—Baerga, Ventura, Kelly, Griffey, Jr., O. Smith, Bonds. **HR**—Sierra, Griffey, Jr., Clark. **SB**—R. Alomar (2). **DNP**—Lee Smith.

LCS

Year	Winner	Loser	Most Valuable Player
1969	Baltimore (E) 3	Minnesota (W) 0	
1970	Baltimore (E) 3	Minnesota (W) 0	
1971	Baltimore (E) 3	Oakland (W) 3	
1972	Oakland (W) 3	Detroit (E) 2	
1973	Oakland (W) 3	Baltimore (E) 2	
1974	Oakland (W) 3	Baltimore (E) 1	
1975	Boston (E) 3	Oakland (W) 0	
1976	New York (E) 3	Kansas City (W) 2	
1977	New York (E) 3	Kansas City (W) 2	
1978	New York (E) 3	Kansas City (W) 1	
1979	Baltimore (E) 3	California (W) 1	
1980	Kansas City (W) 3	New York (E) 0	Frank White, Kansas City
1981	New York (E) 3	Oakland (W) 0	Graig Nettles, New York
1982	Milwaukee (E) 3	California (W) 2	Fred Lynn, California
1983	Baltimore (E) 3	Chicago (W) 1	Mike Boddicker, Baltimore
1984	Detroit (E) 3	Kansas City (W) 0	Kirk Gibson, Detroit
1985	Kansas City (W) 4	Toronto (E) 3	George Brett, Kansas City
1986	Boston (E) 4	California (W) 3	Marty Barrett, Boston
1987	Minnesota (W) 4	Detroit (E) 1	Gary Gaetti, Minnesota
1988	Oakland (W) 4	Boston (E) 0	Dennis Eckersley, Oakland
1989	Oakland (W) 4	Toronto (E) 1	Rickey Henderson, Oakland
1990	Oakland (W) 4	Boston (E) 0	Dave Stewart, Oakland
1991	Minnesota (W) 4	Toronto (E) 1	Kirby Puckett, Minnesota
1992	Toronto (E) 4	Oakland (W) 2	Roberto Alomar, Toronto

1992 Linescores

Oakland	030 000 001 — 4 6 1
Toronto	000 011 010 — 3 9 0
Oakland	000 000 001 — 1 6 0
Toronto	000 020 10x — 3 4 0
Toronto	010 110 211 — 7 9 1
Oakland	000 200 21x — 5 13 2
Toronto	010 000 032 01 — 7 17 4
Oakland	005 001 000 00 — 6 12 2
Toronto	000 100 100 — 2 7 3
Oakland	201 030 00x — 6 8 0
Oakland	000 001 010 — 2 7 1
Toronto	204 010 02x — 9 13 0

WORLD SERIES

Year	Winner	Loser	Year	Winner	Loser
1903	**Boston**, 5	Pittsburgh, 3	1951	**New York**, 4	New York, 2
1905	New York, 4	**Philadelphia**, 1	1952	**New York**, 4	Brooklyn, 3
1906	**Chicago**, 4	Chicago, 2	1953	**New York**, 4	Brooklyn, 2
1907	Chicago, 4	**Detroit**, 1 tie	1954	New York, 4	**Cleveland**, 0
1908	Chicago, 4	**Detroit**, 1	1955	Brooklyn, 4	**New York**, 3
1909	Pittsburgh, 4	**Detroit**, 3	1956	**New York**, 4	Brooklyn, 3
1910	**Phil.**, 4	Chicago, 1	1957	Milwaukee, 4	**New York**, 3
1911	**Phil.**, 4	New York, 2	1958	**New York**, 4	Milwaukee, 3
1912	**Boston**, 4	New York, 3,1 tie	1959	Los Angeles, 4	**Chicago**, 2
1913	**Phil.**, 4	New York, 1	1960	Pittsburgh, 4	**New York**, 3
1914	Boston, 4	**Philadelphia**, 0	1961	**New York**, 4	Cincinnati, 1
1915	**Boston**, 4	Philadelphia, 1	1962	**New York**, 4	San Francisco, 3
1916	**Boston**, 4	Brooklyn, 1	1963	Los Angeles, 4	**New York**, 0
1917	**Chicago**, 4	New York, 2	1964	St. Louis, 4	**New York**, 3
1918	**Boston**, 4	Chicago, 2	1965	Los Angeles, 4	**Minnesota**, 3
1919	Cincinnati, 5	**Chicago**, 3	1966	**Baltimore**, 4	Los Angeles, 0
1920	**Cleveland**, 5	Brooklyn, 2	1967	St. Louis, 4	**Boston**, 3
1921	New York, 5	**New York**, 3	1968	**Detroit**, 4	St. Louis, 3
1922	New York, 4	**New York**, 1 tie	1969	New York, 4	**Baltimore**, 1
1923	**New York**, 4	New York, 2	1970	**Baltimore**, 4	Cincinnati, 1
1924	**Washington**, 4	New York, 3	1971	Pittsburgh, 4	**Baltimore**, 3
1925	Pittsburgh, 4	**Washington**, 3	1972	**Oakland**, 4	Cincinnati, 3
1926	St. Louis, 4	**New York**, 3	1973	**Oakland**, 4	New York, 3
1927	**New York**, 4	Pittsburgh, 0	1974	**Oakland**, 4	Los Angeles, 1
1928	**New York**, 4	St. Louis, 0	1975	Cincinnati, 4	**Boston**, 3
1929	**Phil.**, 4	Chicago, 1	1976	Cincinnati, 4	**New York**, 0
1930	**Phil.**, 4	St. Louis, 2	1977	**New York**, 4	Los Angeles, 2
1931	St. Louis, 4	**Philadelphia**, 3	1978	**New York**, 4	Los Angeles, 2
1932	**New York**, 4	Chicago, 0	1979	Pittsburgh, 4	**Baltimore**, 3
1933	New York, 4	**Washington**, 1	1980	Philadelphia, 4	**Kansas City**, 2
1934	St. Louis, 4	**Detroit**, 3	1981	Los Angeles, 4	**New York**, 2
1935	**Detroit**, 4	Chicago, 2	1982	St. Louis, 4	**Milwaukee**, 3
1936	**New York**, 4	New York, 2	1983	**Baltimore**, 4	Philadelphia, 1
1937	**New York**, 4	New York, 1	1984	**Detroit**, 4	San Diego, 1
1938	**New York**, 4	Chicago, 0	1985	**KC**, 4	St. Louis, 3
1939	**New York**, 4	Cincinnati, 0	1986	New York, 4	**Boston**, 3
1940	Cincinnati, 4	**Detroit**, 3	1987	**Minnesota**, 4	St. Louis, 3
1941	**New York**, 4	Brooklyn, 1	1988	Los Angeles, 4	**Oakland**, 1
1942	St. Louis, 4	**New York**, 1	1989	**Oakland**, 4	San Francisco, 0
1943	**New York**, 4	St. Louis, 1	1990	Cincinnati, 4	**Oakland**, 0
1944	St. Louis, 4	**St. Louis**, 2	1991	**Minnesota**, 4	Atlanta, 3
1945	**Detroit**, 4	Chicago, 3	1992	**Toronto**, 4	Atlanta, 2
1946	St. Louis, 4	**Boston**, 3			
1947	**New York**, 4	Brooklyn, 3			
1948	**Cleveland**, 4	Boston, 2	American League teams are in bold.		
1949	**New York**, 4	Brooklyn, 1			
1950	**New York**, 4	Philadelphia, 0			

1992 WORLD SERIES

Game 1
Toronto   000 100 000—1 4 0
Atlanta   000 003 00x—3 4 0
LOB: Toronto 2, Atlanta 7. **HR**—Berryhill (1), Carter (1). **RBI**—Carter (1), Berryhill 3 (3). **SB**—Nixon (1), Gant (1).

Game 2
Toronto   000 020 012—5 9 2
Atlanta   010 120 00x—4 5 1
LOB: Toronto 6, Atlanta 8. **2B**—Alomar (1), Borders (1). **HR**—Sprague (1). **RBI**—White (1), Winfield (1), Cone (1), Sprague 2 (2), Justice (1), Hunter (1), Lemke (1). **SB**—Sanders 2 (2), Justice (1), Blauser (1), Gant (2). **SF**—Hunter.

Game 3
Atlanta   000 001 010—2 9 0
Toronto   000 100 011—3 6 1
E—Gruber (1). **LOB:** Atlanta 6, Toronto 5. **2B**—Sanders (1). **HR**—Carter (2), Gruber (1). **RBI**—Justice (2), LSmith (1), Carter (2), Maldonado (1), Gruber (1). **SB**—Nixon (2), Sanders (3), Alomar (2), Gruber (1).

Game 4
Atlanta   000 000 010—1 5 0
Toronto   001 000 10x—2 6 0
LOB: Atlanta 4, Toronto 5. **2B**—Gant (1), White (1). **HR**—Borders (1). **RBI**—Lemke (2), White (2), Borders (1). **SB**—Nixon (3), Blauser (2), Alomar (2).

Game 5
Atlanta   100 150 000—7 13 0
Toronto   010 100 000—2 6 1
LOB: Atlanta 5, Toronto 7. **2B**—Nixon (1), Pendleton 2 (2), Borders (2). **HR**—Justice (1), LSmith (1). **RBI**—Sanders (1), Pendleton (1), Justice (3), LSmith 4 (5), Borders 2 (3). **SB**—Nixon 2 (5).

Game 6
Toronto   100 100 000 02—4 14 1
Atlanta   001 000 001 01—3 8 1
LOB: Toronto 13, Atlanta 10. **2B**—Carter 2 (2), Winfield (1), Borders (3), Sanders (2). **HR**—Maldonado (1)). **RBI**—Carter (3), Winfield 2 (3), Maldonado (2), Nixon (1), Pendleton (2), Hunter (2). **SB**—White (1), Alomar (3), Sanders 2 (5).
Series MVP: Pat Borders, Toronto

AWARDS

Most Valuable Player
1983 Cal Ripken, Jr., Baltimore
1984 Willie Hernandez, Detroit
1985 Don Mattingly, New York
1986 Roger Clemens, Boston
1987 George Bell, Toronto
1988 Jose Canseco, Oakland
1989 Robin Yount, Milwaukee
1990 Rickey Henderson, Oakland
1991 Cal Ripken, Jr., Baltimore
1992 Dennis Eckersley, Boston

Cy Young
1983 LaMarr Hoyt, Chicago
1984 Willie Hernandez, Detroit
1985 Bret Saberhagen, Kansas City
1986 Roger Clemens, Boston
1987 Roger Clemens, Boston
1988 Frank Viola, Minnesota
1989 Bret Saberhagen, Kansas City
1990 Bob Welch, Oakland
1991 Roger Clemens, Boston
1992 Dennis Eckersley, Boston

Rookie of the Year
1983 Ron Kittle, Chicago
1984 Alvin Davis, Seattle
1985 Ozzie Guillen, Oakland
1986 Jose Canseco, Oakland
1987 Mark McGwire, Oakland
1988 Walt Weiss, Oakland
1989 Gregg Olson, Baltimore
1990 Sandy Alomar Jr., Cleveland
1991 Chuck Knoblauch, Minnesota
1992 Pat Listash, Milwaukee

Manager of the Year
1983 Tony La Russa, Chicago
1984 Sparky Anderson, Detroit
1985 Bobby Cox, Toronto
1986 John McNamara, Boston
1987 Sparky Anderson, Detroit
1988 Tony La Russa, Oakland
1989 Frank Robinson, Baltimore
1990 Jeff Torborg, Chicago
1991 Tom Kelly, Minnesota
1992 Tony La Russa, Oakland

Rawlings Gold Glove Awards 1992
1B Don Mattingly, New York
2B Roberto Alomar, Toronto
3B Robin Ventura, Chicago
SS Cal Ripken, Jr., Baltimore
OF Ken Griffey, Jr., Seattle
OF Devon White, Toronto
OF Kirby Puckett, Minnesota
P   Mark Langston, California
C   Ivan Rodriguez, Texas

Rawlings Gold Glove All-Time Team
1B George Scott
2B Frank White
3B Brooks Robinson
SS Luis Aparacio
OF Al Kaline
OF Dwight Evans
OF Paul Blair
P   Jim Kaat
C   Jim Sundberg

1993 MILESTONES

Games

Player	Has	Needs	Milestone
Robin Yount	2,729	71	2,800
Dave Winfield	2,707	93	2,800
George Brett	2,562	38	2,600
Carlton Fisk	2,474	26	2,500
Eddie Murray	2,444	56	2,500

At Bats

Player	Has	Needs	Milestone
Robin Yount	10,554	101	10,655 to pass Brooks Robinson into 7th place
		328	10,882 to pass Willie Mays into 6th place
		418	10,972 to pass Stan Musial into 5th place
Dave Winfield	10,047	32	10,079 to pass Walter Maranville into 14th place
		70	10,117 to pass Al Kaline into 13th place
		162	10,209 to pass Tris Speaker into 12th place
		184	10,231 to pass Luis Aparicio into 11th place
		286	10,333 to pass Lou Brock into 10th place
		395	10,442 to pass Honus Wagner into 9th place
George Brett	9,789	211	10,000
Eddie Murray	9,124	76	9,200

Hits

Player	Has	Needs	Milestone
Robin Yount	3,025	29	3,054 to pass Rod Carew into 13th place
		57	3,082 to pass Cap Anson into 12th place
		118	3,153 to pass Paul Waner into 11th place
George Brett	3,005	3	3,008 to pass Al Kaline into 16th place
		18	3,023 to pass Lou Brock into 15th place
Dave Winfield	2,866	134	3,000

Singles

Player	Has	Needs	Milestone
Robin Yount	2,101	99	2,200
George Brett	1,939	61	2,000
Dave Winfield	1,858	42	1,900
Willie Randolph	1,775	25	1,800

Doubles

Player	Has	Needs	Milestone
George Brett	634	13	647 to pass Carl Yastrzemski into 7th place
		18	652 to pass Honus Wagner into 6th place
		19	653 to pass Nap Lajoie into 5th place
Robin Yount	558	17	575 to pass Charlie Gehringer into 11th place
		47	605 to pass Paul Waner into 10th place
Dave Winfield	493	7	500

1993 MILESTONES

Triples

Player	Has	Needs	Milestone
Willie Wilson	142	8	150
George Brett	134	16	150
Robin Yount	123	27	150
Tim Raines	96	4	100
Andre Dawson	94	6	100
Dave Winfield	83	17	100

Home Runs

Player	Has	Needs	Milestone
Davie Winfield	432	18	450
Eddie Murray	414	36	450
Andre Dawson	399	1	400
Dale Murphy	398	2	400
Carlton Fisk	375	25	400

Grand Slams

Player	Has	Needs	Milestone
Eddie Murray	17	1	18 to tie Willie McCovey for 2nd place

Runs Batted In

Player	Has	Needs	Milestone
Dave Winfield	1,710	103	1,813 to pass Frank Robinson into 12th place
Eddie Murray	1,562	38	1,600
George Brett	1,520	80	1,600
Andre Dawson	1,425	75	1,500

Stolen Bases

Player	Has	Needs	Milestone
Rickey Henderson	1,042		extending his major league record
Tim Raines	730	9	739 to pass Max Carey into 5th place
		14	744 to pass Eddie Collins into 4th place
Willie Wilson	650	40	690 to pass Joe Morgan into 8th place
Vince Coleman	610	40	650 to pass Bert Campaneris into 9th place
Ozzie Smith	542	9	551 to pass Cesar Cedeno into 26th place

Victories

Player	Has	Needs	Milestone
Nolan Ryan	319	6	325 to pass Don Sutton into 11th place
		8	327 to pass John Clarkson into 10th place
		11	330 to pass Steve Carlton into 9th place
Bert Blyleven	287	2	289 to pass Tommy John into 21st place
		13	300

Strikeouts

Player	Has	Needs	Milestone
Nolan Ryan	5,668	32	5,700 extending his major league record

1993 MILESTONES

Player	Has	Needs	Milestone
Bert Blyleven	3,701	299	4,000 to pass Tom Seaver into 3rd place
Frank Tanana	2,657	163	2,820 to pass Cy Young into 13th place
		176	2,833 to pass Mickey Lolich into 12th place
		199	2,856 to pass Jim Bunning into 11th place

Shutouts

Player	Has	Needs	Milestone
Nolan Ryan	61	1	62 to pass Tom Seaver into 7th place
		3	64 to pass Warren Spahn into 6th place
Bert Blyleven	60	2	62 to pass Tom Seaver into 7th place

Innings Pitched

Player	Has	Needs	Milestone
Nolan Ryan	5,321	33	5,353 to pass Gaylord Perry into 5th place
		83	5,404 to pass Phil Niekro into 4th place
		602	5,923 to pass Walter Johnson into 3rd place
Bert Blyleven	4,970	30	5,000
		74	5,044 to pass Tim Keefe into 12th place
		98	5,068 to pass Charlie Nichols into 11th place
		119	5,189 to pass Grover Alexander into 10th place

Games Pitched

Player	Has	Needs	Milestone
Jeff Reardon	811	14	825 to pass Frank McGraw into 11th place
		46	849 to pass Elroy Face into 10th place
Charlie Hough	803		Same as above
Nolan Ryan	794	9	803 to pass Walter Johnson into 14th place
Lee Smith	787	13	800
Dennis Eckersley	740	60	800

Saves

Player	Has	Needs	Milestone
Jeff Reardon	357		extending his major league record
Lee Smith	355		
Dave Righetti	251	50	301 to pass Bruce Sutter into 5th place
Dennis Eckersley	239	6	245 to pass Dan Quisenberry into 7th place
John Franco	226	19	245 to pass Dan Quisenberry into 7th place
Tom Henke	220	3	223 to pass Sparky Lyke into 8th place
Dave Smith	216	3	219 to pass Gene Garber into 9th place
		7	223 to pass Sparky Lyle into 8th place
		29	245 to pass Dan Quisenberry into 7th place
Bobby Thigpen	200	19	219 to pass Gene Garber into 12th place

Managers—Victories

Manager	Has	Needs	Milestone
Sparky Anderson	1,996	15	2,011 to pass Leo Durocher into 6th place

1992 MINOR LEAGUE RESULTS

American Association (AAA)
East

Team (Club)	W	L	PCT.	GB
Buffalo (Pitt)	87	57	.604	—
Indianapolis (Mon)	83	61	.576	4
Louisville (StL)	73	70	.510	13.5
Nashville (Cin)	67	77	.465	20

West

Team (Club)	W	L	PCT.	GB
Ok. City (Tex)	74	70	.514	—
Denver (Mil)	73	71	.507	1
Omaha (KC)	67	77	.465	7
Iowa (Chi)	51	92	.357	22.5

International League (AAA)
East

Team (Club)	W	L	PCT.	GB
Scranton/Wilkes-Barre (Phil)	84	58	.592	—
Pawtucket (Bos)	71	72	.497	13.5
Rochester (Bal)	70	74	.486	15
Syracuse (Tor)	60	83	.420	24.5

West

Team (Club)	W	L	PCT.	GB
Columbus (NYY)	95	49	.660	—
Richmond (Atl)	73	71	.507	22
Toledo (Det)	64	80	.444	31
Tidewater (NYM)	56	86	.394	38

Pacific Coast League (AAA)
Overall

Team (Club)	W	L	PCT.	GB
Colorado Springs (Cle)	84	57	.596	—
Portland (Min)	83	61	.576	2.5
Vancouver (CWS)	81	61	.570	3.5
Edmonton (Cal)	74	69	.517	11
Las Vegas (SD)	74	70	.514	11.5
Tucson (Hou)	70	74	.486	15.5
Phoenix (SF)	66	78	.458	19.5
Albuquerque (LA)	65	78	.455	20
Calgary (Sea)	60	78	.435	22.5
Tacoma (Oak)	56	87	.392	29

1992 MINOR LEAGUE RESULTS

Eastern League (AA)

Team (Club)	W	L	PCT.	GB
Canton-Akron (Cle)	80	58	.580	—
Binghamton (NYM)	79	59	.572	1
Harrisburg (Mon)	78	59	.569	1.5
Albany-Colonie (NYY)	71	68	.511	9.5
London (Det)	67	70	.489	12.5
Reading (Phil)	61	77	.442	19
Hagerstown (Bal)	59	80	.424	21.5
New Britain (Bos)	58	82	.414	23

Southern League (AA)
Overall

Team (Club)	W	L	PCT.	GB
Greenville (Atl)	100	43	.699	—
Chattanooga (Cin)	90	53	.629	10
Huntsville (Oak)	81	63	.563	19.5
Memphis (KC)	71	73	.493	29.5
Charlotte (Chi)	70	73	.490	30
Birmingham (CWS)	68	74	.479	31.5
Jacksonville (Sea)	68	75	.476	32
Orlando (Min)	60	82	.423	39.5
Knoxville (Tor)	56	88	.389	44.5
Carolina (Pitt)	52	92	.361	48.5

Texas League (AA)
Overall

Team (Club)	W	L	PCT.	GB
Shreveport (SF)	77	59	.566	—
Tulsa (Tex)	77	59	.566	—
El Paso (Mil)	73	63	.537	4
Wichita (SD)	70	66	.515	7
Midland (Cal)	61	72	.459	14.5
San Antonio (LA)	62	74	.456	15
Jackson (Hou)	61	74	.452	15.5
Arkansas (StL)	59	73	.447	16

1992 INDIVIDUAL LEADERS

Batting Average

Martinez, E	SEA	.343
Puckett, K	MIN	.329
Thomas, F	CWS	.323
Molitor, P	MIL	.320
Mack, S	MIN	.315
Baerga, C	CLE	.312
Alomar, R	TOR	.310
Griffey Jr, K	SEA	.308
Harper, B	MIN	.307
Bordick, M	OAK	.300

Home Runs

Gonzalez, J	TEX	43
McGwire, M	OAK	42
Fielder, C	DET	35
Belle, A	CLE	34
Carter, J	TOR	34
Deer, R	DET	32
Tettleton, M	DET	32
Griffey Jr, K	SEA	27
3 Players tied		26

Runs Batted In

Fielder, C	DET	124
Carter, J	TOR	119
Thomas, F	CWS	115
Belle, A	CLE	112
Bell, G	CWS	112
Puckett, K	MIN	110
Gonzalez, J	TEX	109
Winfield, D	TOR	108
Devereaux, M	BAL	107
Baerga, C	CLE	105

Runs

Phillips, T	DET	114
Thomas, F	CWS	108
Alomar, R	TOR	105
Knoblauch, C	MIN	104
Puckett, K	MIN	104
Raines, T	CWS	102
Mack, S	MIN	101
Anderson, B	BAL	100
Martinez, E	SEA	100
White, D	TOR	98

Hits

Puckett, K	MIN	210
Baerga, C	CLE	205
Molitor, P	MIL	195
Mack, S	MIN	189
Thomas, F	CWS	185
Mattingly, D	NYY	184
Martinez, E	SEA	181
Devereaux, M	BAL	180
Knoblauch, C	MIN	178
Alomar, R	TOR	177

Total Bases

Puckett, K	MIN	313
Carter, J	TOR	310
Gonzalez, J	TEX	309
Thomas, F	CWS	307
Devereaux, M	BAL	303
Griffey Jr, K	SEA	302
Baerga, C	CLE	299
Martinez, E	SEA	287
Winfield, D	TOR	286
Molitor, P	MIL	281

Stolen Bases

Lofton, K	CLE	66
Listach, P	MIL	54
Anderson, B	BAL	53
Polonia, L	CAL	51
Alomar, R	TOR	49
Henderson, R	OAK	48
Raines, T	CWS	45
Curtis, C	CAL	43
Hamilton, D	MIL	41
Johnson, L	CWS	41

1992 INDIVIDUAL LEADERS

Hitting Streaks

25	Johnson, L	CWS
07/16 - 08/11		
22	Mack, S	MIN
07/26 - 08/18		
19	Thomas, F	CWS
07/20 - 08/09		
18	Jefferies, G	KC
05/13 - 06/01		
17	5 Players tied	

Walks

Thomas, F	CWS	122
Tettleton, M	DET	122
Phillips, T	DET	114
Milligan, R	BAL	106
Tartabull, D	NYY	103
Anderson, B	BAL	98
Henderson, R	OAK	95
Ventura, R	CWS	93
McGwire, M	OAK	90
Knoblauch, C	MIN	88

Slugging Percentage

McGwire, M	OAK	.585
Martinez, E	SEA	.544
Thomas, F	CWS	.536
Griffey Jr, K	SEA	.535
Gonzalez, J	TEX	.529
Carter, J	TOR	.498
Winfield, D	TOR	.491
Puckett, K	MIN	.490
Tartabull, D	NYY	.489
Belle, A	CLE	.477

Earned Run Average

Clemens, R	BOS	2.41
Appier, K	KC	2.46
Mussina, M	BAL	2.54
Guzman, J	TOR	2.64
Abbott, J	CAL	2.77
Perez, M	NYY	2.87
Nagy, C	CLE	2.96
McDowell, J	CWS	3.18
Wegman, B	MIL	3.20
Smiley, J	MIN	3.21

Wins

Brown, K	TEX	21
Morris, J	TOR	21
McDowell, J	CWS	20
Mussina, M	BAL	18
Clemens, R	BOS	18
Fleming, D	SEA	17
Nagy, C	CLE	17
Navarro, J	MIL	17
Moore, M	OAK	17
6 Players tied		16

Winning Streaks

Eldred, C	MIL	10
08/08 - 09/29		
Bosio, C	MIL	10
07/25 - 09/24		
Fleming, D	SEA	9
04/15 - 06/09		
Appier, K	KC	9
05/30 - 07/29		
Morris, J	TOR	8
05/31 - 07/21		

Saves

Eckersley, D	OAK	51
Aguilera, R	MIN	41
Montgomery, J	KC	39
Olson, G	BAL	36
Henke, T	TOR	34

1992 INDIVIDUAL LEADERS

Russell,J	OAK	30
Farr,S	NYY	30
Olin,S	CLE	29
Henry,D	MIL	29
Reardon,J	BOS	27

Games Started

Sutcliffe,R	BAL	36
Moore,M	OAK	36
McDonald,B	BAL	35
Brown,K	TEX	35
Wegman,B	MIL	35
Viola,F	BOS	35
7 Players tied		34

Complete Games

McDowell,J	CWS	13
Brown,K	TEX	11
Clemens,R	BOS	11
Nagy,C	CLE	10
Perez,M	NYY	10
Langston,M	CAL	9
Mussina,M	BAL	8
Fleming,D	SEA	7
Abbott,J	CAL	7
Wegman,B	MIL	7

Innings Pitched

Brown,K	TEX	265.2
Wegman,B	MIL	261.2
McDowell,J	CWS	260.2
Nagy,C	CLE	252.0
Perez,M	NYY	247.2
Clemens,R	BOS	246.2
Navarro,J	MIL	246.0
Mussina,M	BAL	241.0
Smiley,J	MIN	241.0
Morris,J	TOR	240.2

Strikeouts

Johnson,R	SEA	241
Perez,M	NYY	218
Clemens,R	BOS	208
Guzman,J	TEX	179
McDowell,J	CWS	178
Langston,M	CAL	174
Brown,K	TEX	173
Nagy,C	CLE	169
Guzman,J	TOR	165
Smiley,J	MIN	163

Winning Percentage

Mussina,M	BAL	(18-05)	.783
Morris,J	TOR	(21-06)	.778
Guzman,J	TOR	(16-05)	.762
Bosio,C	MIL	(16-06)	.727
McDowell,J	CWS	(20-10)	.667
Brown,K	TEX	(21-11)	.656
Appier,K	KC	(15-08)	.652
Smiley,J	MIN	(16-09)	.640
Fleming,D	SEA	(17-10)	.630
Nagy,C	CLE	(17-10)	.630

Op. Batting Average Against

Johnson,R	SEA	.206
Guzman,J	TOR	.207
Appier,K	KC	.217
Clemens,R	BOS	.224
Smiley,J	MIN	.231
Perez,M	NYY	.235
Stewart,D	OAK	.237
Mussina,M	BAL	.239

BALTIMORE ORIOLES

Club Records (since 1900)

Batting

Batting	Ken Singleton	.328
Hitting streak	Eddie Murray	22
Home runs	Frank Robinson	49
RBI	Jim Gentile	141
Hits	Cal Ripken, Jr.	211
Runs	Frank Robinson	122
Doubles	Cal Ripken, Jr.	47
Triples	Paul Blair	12
Stolen bases	Luis Aparicio	57
Bases on balls	Ken Singleton	118
Strikeouts (most)	Mickey Tettleton	160

Pitching

Games (appearances)	Tippy Martinez	76
Complete games	Jim Palmer	25
Innings pitched	Jim Palmer	323
Games won	Steve Stone	25
Games lost	Don Larsen	21
Games started	Mike Cuellar, Jim Palmer, Mike Flanagan	40
Games finished	Gregg Olson	62
Bases on balls	Bob Turley	181
Strikeouts	Dave McNally	202
Saves	Gregg Olson	37

BALTIMORE ORIOLES

1992 Roster

PLAYER	AVG	G	AB	R	H	HR	RBI	BB	SO	SB
+Alexander,M	.200	4	5	1	1	0	0	0	3	0
Anderson,B	.271	159	623	100	169	21	80	98	98	53
Davis,G	.276	106	398	46	110	13	48	37	65	1
Dempsey,R	.111	8	9	2	1	0	0	2	1	0
Devereaux,M	.276	156	653	76	180	24	107	44	94	10
Gomez,L	.265	137	468	62	124	17	64	63	78	2
Hoiles,C	.274	96	310	49	85	20	40	55	60	0
Horn,S	.235	63	162	13	38	5	19	21	60	0
Hulett,T	.289	57	142	11	41	2	21	10	31	0
Martinez,C	.268	83	198	26	53	5	25	31	47	0
McLemore,M	.246	101	228	40	56	0	27	21	26	11
RIGHT	.276		58		16	0	10	5	9	
LEFT	.235		170		40	0	17	16	17	
+Mercedes,L	.140	23	50	7	7	0	4	8	9	0
Milligan,R	.240	137	462	71	111	11	53	106	81	0
Orsulak,J	.289	117	391	45	113	4	39	28	34	5
Parent,M	.235	17	34	4	8	2	4	3	7	0
Ripken Jr,C	.251	162	637	73	160	14	72	64	50	4
Ripken,B	.230	111	330	35	76	4	36	18	26	2
+Scarsone,S	.176	11	17	2	3	0	0	1	6	0
Segui,D	.233	115	189	21	44	1	17	20	23	1
RIGHT	.205		78		16	0	9	7	14	
LEFT	.252		111		28	1	8	13	9	
+Shields,T	.000	2	0	0	0	0	0	0	0	0
+Tackett,J	.240	65	179	21	43	5	24	17	28	0
+Voigt,J	.000	1	0	0	0	0	0	0	0	0
BALTIMORE	.259	162	5485	705	1423	148	680	647	827	89
OPPONENTS	.257	162	5531	656	1419	124	626	518	846	131
DH	.262	162	626	74	164	19	74	65	142	4

BALTIMORE ORIOLES

1992 Roster

PITCHER	R/L	W	L	ERA	G	GS	SV	BB	SO	OP. AVG
Clements,P	L	2	0	3.28	23	0	0	11	9	.258
Davis,S	R	7	3	3.43	48	2	4	36	53	.244
Flanagan,M	L	0	0	8.05	42	0	0	23	17	.338
Frohwirth,T	R	4	3	2.46	65	0	4	41	58	.247
Lefferts,C	L	1	3	4.09	5	5	0	6	23	.268
+Lewis,R	R	1	1	10.80	2	2	0	7	4	.406
McDonald,B	R	13	13	4.24	35	35	0	74	158	.247
Mesa,J	R	7	12	4.59	28	27	0	70	62	.273
Milacki,B	R	6	8	5.84	23	20	1	44	51	.297
Mills,A	R	10	4	2.61	35	3	2	54	60	.215
Mussina,M	R	18	5	2.54	32	32	0	48	130	.239
Olson,G	R	1	5	2.05	60	0	36	24	58	.211
Poole,J	L	0	0	0.00	6	0	0	1	3	.231
+Rhodes,A	L	7	5	3.63	15	15	0	38	77	.250
Sutcliffe,R	R	16	15	4.47	36	36	0	74	109	.273
Williamson,M	R	0	0	0.96	12	0	1	10	14	.239
BALTIMORE		89	73	3.79	162	162	48	518	846	.257
OPPONENTS		73	89	4.15	162	162	39	647	827	.259

Key: +Rookie   *Player on the disabled list at the end of the season

Stadium: Oriole Park at Camden Yards
Capacity: 48,000
Oriole Park at Camden Yards
333 W. Camden Street
Baltimore, MD 21201
General tel. number: (410) 685-9800
Credit card orders: (410) 481-SEAT; (202) 432-SEAT; (703) 573-SEAT
Group and corporate sales: (410) 547-6600/6601
1993 Ticket Prices
 Box: $11–14
 Reserved: $6–8
 Club: $15–25
 Bleachers: $4
 Sr. citizens, children: $1

CONTACT & TICKET INFORMATION

BOSTON RED SOX

Club Records (since 1900)

Batting

Batting	Ted Williams	.406
Hitting streak	Dom DiMaggio	34
Home runs	Jimmie Foxx	50
RBI	Jimmie Foxx	175
Hits	Wade Boggs	240
Runs	Ted Williams	150
Doubles	Earl Webb	67
Triples	Chick Stahl, Tris Speaker	22
Stolen bases	Tommy Harper	54
Bases on balls	Ted Williams	162
Strikeouts (most)	Butch Hobson	162

Pitching

Games (appearances)	Dick Radatz	79
Complete games	Cy Young	41
Innings pitched	Cy Young	386
Games won	Joe Wood	34
Games lost	Charley Ruffing	25
Games started	Cy Young	43
Games finished	Dick Radatz	67
Bases on balls	Mel Parnell	134
Strikeouts	Roger Clemens	291
Saves	Jeff Reardon	40

BOSTON RED SOX

1992 Roster

PLAYER	AVG	G	AB	R	H	HR	RBI	BB	SO	SB
+Barrett,T	.000	4	3	1	0	0	0	2	0	0
RIGHT	.000		0		0	0	0	0	0	
LEFT	.000		3		0	0	0	2	0	
Boggs,W	.259	143	514	62	133	7	50	74	31	1
Brumley,M	.000	2	1	0	0	0	0	0	0	0
RIGHT	.000		0		0	0	0	0	0	
LEFT	.000		1		0	0	0	0	0	
Brunansky,T	.266	138	458	47	122	15	74	66	96	2
*Burks,E	.255	66	235	35	60	8	30	25	48	5
Clark,J	.210	81	257	32	54	5	33	56	87	1
+Cooper,S	.276	123	337	34	93	5	33	37	33	1
+Flaherty,J	.197	35	66	3	13	0	2	3	7	0
*Greenwell,M	.233	49	180	16	42	2	18	18	19	2
Hatcher,B	.238	75	315	37	75	1	23	17	41	4
Lyons,S	.250	21	28	3	7	0	2	2	1	0
Marzano,J	.080	19	50	4	4	0	1	2	12	0
Naehring,T	.231	72	186	12	43	3	14	18	31	0
Pena,T	.241	133	410	39	99	1	38	24	61	3
Plantier,P	.246	108	349	46	86	7	30	44	83	2
Reed,J	.247	143	550	64	136	3	40	62	44	7
Rivera,L	.215	102	288	17	62	0	29	26	56	4
+Valentin,J	.276	58	185	21	51	5	25	20	17	1
Vaughn,M	.234	113	355	42	83	13	57	47	67	3
+Wedge,E	.250	27	68	11	17	5	11	13	18	0
Winningham,H	.235	105	234	27	55	1	14	10	53	6
+Zupcic,R	.276	124	392	46	108	3	43	25	60	2
BOSTON	.246	162	5461	599	1343	84	567	591	865	44
OPPONENTS	.255	162	5496	669	1403	107	621	535	943	115
DH	.235	162	592	76	139	16	69	85	132	3

BOSTON RED SOX

1992 Roster

PITCHER	R/L	W	L	ERA	G	GS	SV	BB	SO	OP.AVG
Bolton,T	L	1	2	3.41	21	1	0	14	23	.286
Clemens,R	R	18	11	2.41	32	32	0	62	208	.224
Darwin,D	R	9	9	3.96	51	15	3	53	124	.257
Dopson,J	R	7	11	4.08	25	25	0	38	55	.287
Fossas,T	L	1	2	2.43	60	0	2	14	19	.279
Gardiner,M	R	4	10	4.75	28	18	0	58	79	.253
Harris,G	R	4	9	2.51	70	2	4	60	73	.215
Hesketh,J	L	8	9	4.36	30	25	1	58	104	.276
+Hoy,P	R	0	0	7.36	5	0	0	2	2	.471
Irvine,D	R	3	4	6.11	21	0	0	14	10	.287
+Quantrill,P	R	2	3	2.19	27	0	1	15	24	.288
Reardon,J	R	2	2	4.25	46	0	27	7	32	.308
+Ryan,K	R	0	0	6.43	7	0	1	5	5	.174
+Taylor,S	L	1	1	4.91	4	1	0	4	7	.245
Viola,F	L	13	12	3.44	35	35	0	89	121	.242
Young,M	L	0	4	4.58	28	8	0	42	57	.257
BOSTON		73	89	3.58	162	162	39	535	943	.255
OPPONENTS		89	73	3.39	162	162	51	591	865	.246

Key: +Rookie *Player on the disabled list at the end of the season

CONTACT & TICKET INFORMATION

Stadium: Fenway Park
Capacity: 33,925
4 Yawkey Way
Boston, MA 02215
General tel. number: (617) 267-9440
Tickets: (617) 267-8661
Credit card orders: (617) 267-1700
Group, corporate sales: (617) 262-1915
1993 Ticket Prices
    Box: $14–18
    Reserved: $10
    Bleachers: $7

CALIFORNIA ANGELS

Club Records (since 1900)

Batting

Batting	Rod Carew	.339
Hitting streak	Rod Carew	25
Home runs	Reggie Jackson	39
RBI	Don Baylor	139
Hits	Alex Johnson	202
Runs	Don Baylor	120
Doubles	Doug DeCinces, Johnny Ray	42
Triples	Jim Fregosi, Mickey Rivers	13
Stolen bases	Mickey Rivers	70
Bases on balls	Brain Downing	106
Strikeouts (most)	Reggie Jackson	156

Pitching

Games (appearances)	Minnie Rojas	72
Complete games	Nolan Ryan	26
Innings pitched	Nolan Ryan	333
Games won	Clyde Wright, Nolan Ryan	22
Games lost	George Brunet, Clyde Wright, Frank Tanana, Kirk McCaskill	19
Games started	Nolan Ryan	41
Games finished	Bryan Harvey	63
Bases on balls	Nolan Ryan	204
Strikeouts	Nolan Ryan	383
Saves	Bryan Harvey	46

CALIFORNIA ANGELS

1992 Roster

PLAYER	AVG	G	AB	R	H	HR	RBI	BB	SO	SB
Brooks,H	.216	82	306	28	66	8	36	12	46	3
+Curtis,C	.259	139	441	59	114	10	46	51	71	43
Davis,A	.250	40	104	5	26	0	16	13	9	0
+DiSarcina,G	.247	157	518	48	128	3	42	20	50	9
Ducey,R	.188	54	80	7	15	0	2	5	22	2
+Easley,D	.258	47	151	14	39	1	12	8	26	9
Felix,J	.246	139	509	63	125	9	72	33	128	8
RIGHT	.271		118		32	3	18	3	30	
LEFT	.238		391		93	6	54	30	98	
Fitzgerald,M	.212	95	189	19	40	6	17	22	34	2
Gaetti,G	.226	130	456	41	103	12	48	21	79	3
*Gonzales,R	.277	104	329	47	91	7	38	41	46	7
Gonzalez,J	.182	33	55	4	10	0	2	7	20	0
Hayes,V	.225	94	307	35	69	4	29	37	54	11
Langston,M	.000	33	2	1	0	0	0	0	2	0
Morris,J	.193	43	57	4	11	1	3	4	11	1
*Myers,G	.231	30	78	4	18	1	13	5	11	0
Oberkfell,K	.264	41	91	6	24	0	10	8	5	0
Orton,J	.219	43	114	11	25	2	12	7	32	1
Parrish,L	.233	93	275	26	64	12	32	24	70	1
Polonia,L	.286	149	577	83	165	0	35	45	64	51
Rose,B	.214	30	84	10	18	2	10	8	9	1
+Salmon,T	.177	23	79	8	14	2	6	11	23	1
Schofield,D	.333	1	3	0	1	0	0	1	0	0
Sojo,L	.272	106	368	37	100	7	43	14	24	7
Stevens,L	.221	106	312	25	69	7	37	29	64	1
Tingley,R	.197	71	127	15	25	3	8	13	35	0
+Williams,R	.231	14	26	5	6	0	2	1	10	0
RIGHT	.250		8		2	0	0	1	3	
LEFT	.222		18		4	0	0	0	7	
CALIFORNIA	.243	162	5364	579	1306	88	537	416	882	160
OPPONENTS	.264	162	5484	671	1449	130	626	532	888	120
DH	.247	162	647	77	160	11	62	34	102	18

CALIFORNIA ANGELS

1992 Roster

PITCHER	R/L	W	L	ERA	G	GS	SV	BB	SO	OP.AVG
Abbott,J	L	7	15	2.77	29	29	0	68	130	.263
Bailes,S	L	3	1	7.45	32	0	0	28	25	.351
Blyleven,B	R	8	12	4.74	25	24	0	29	70	.285
+Butcher,M	R	2	2	3.25	19	0	0	13	24	.264
Crim,C	R	7	6	5.17	57	0	1	29	30	.293
Eichhorn,M	R	4	4	3.08	65	0	2	25	61	.255
Finley,C	L	7	12	3.96	31	31	0	98	124	.278
+Fortugno,T	L	1	1	5.18	14	5	1	19	31	.236
Frey,S	L	4	2	3.57	51	0	4	22	24	.238
Grahe,J	R	5	6	3.52	46	7	21	39	39	.246
*Harvey,B	R	0	4	2.83	25	0	13	11	34	.208
+Hathaway,H	L	0	0	7.94	2	1	0	3	1	.333
Langston,M	L	13	14	3.66	32	32	0	74	174	.242
Lewis,S	R	4	0	3.99	21	2	0	14	18	.255
Robinson,D	R	1	0	2.20	3	3	0	3	9	.292
+Valera,J	R	8	11	3.73	30	28	0	64	113	.262
CALIFORNIA		72	90	3.84	162	162	42	532	888	.264
OPPONENTS		90	72	3.14	162	162	45	416	882	.243

Key: +Rookie *Player on the disabled list at the end of the season

Stadium: Anaheim Stadium
Capacity: 64,593
Box 2000
Anaheim, CA 92803
General tel. number: (714) 634-2000 or (213) 625-1123 or (800) 6AN-GELS
Tickets: (714) 740-2000; (213) 480-3232; (805) 583-8700; (619) 278-PIXS
Credit card orders: (617) 267-1700
Group, corporate sales: (617) 262-1915
1993 Ticket Prices
  Club: $11
  Box: $8
  Reserved: $7
  General: $4
  Children (General, Mon. to Thurs.): $1

CHICAGO WHITE SOX

Club Records (since 1900)

Batting		
Batting	Luke Appling	.388
Hitting streak	Luke Appling	27
Home runs	Dick Allen, Carlton Fisk	37
RBI	Zeke Bonura	138
Hits	Eddie Collins	222
Runs	Johnny Mostil	135
Doubles	Floyd Robinson	45
Triples	Joe Jackson	21
Stolen bases	Rudy Law	77
Bases on balls	Frank Thomas	138
Strikeouts (most)	Dave Nicholson	175

Pitching		
Games (appearances)	Wilbur Wood	88
Complete games	Ed Walsh	42
Innings pitched	Ed Walsh	464
Games won	Ed Walsh	40
Games lost	Pat Flaherty	25
Games started	Ed Walsh, Wilbur Wood	49
Games finished	Bobby Thigpen	73
Bases on balls	Vern Kennedy	147
Strikeouts	Ed Walsh	269
Saves	Bobby Thigpen	57

CHICAGO WHITE SOX

1992 Roster

PLAYER	AVG	G	AB	R	H	HR	RBI	BB	SO	SB
Abner,S	.279	97	208	21	58	1	16	12	35	1
Bell,G	.255	155	627	74	160	25	112	31	97	5
+Beltre,E	.191	49	110	21	21	1	10	3	18	1
Cora,J	.246	68	122	27	30	0	9	22	13	10
RIGHT	.222		27		6	0	3	5	4	
LEFT	.253		95		24	0	6	17	9	
+Cron,C	.000	6	10	0	0	0	0	0	4	0
Fisk,C	.229	62	188	12	43	3	21	23	38	3
*Grebeck,C	.268	88	287	24	77	3	35	30	34	0
*Guillen,O	.200	12	40	5	8	0	7	1	5	1
Hemond,S	.225	25	40	8	9	0	2	4	13	1
Huff,M	.209	60	115	13	24	0	8	10	24	1
+Jeter,S	.111	13	18	1	2	0	0	0	7	0
Johnson,L	.279	157	567	67	158	3	47	34	33	41
Karkovice,R	.237	123	342	39	81	13	50	30	89	10
Merullo,M	.180	24	50	3	9	0	3	1	8	0
Newson,W	.221	63	136	19	30	1	11	37	38	3
Pasqua,D	.211	93	265	26	56	6	33	36	57	0
Raines,T	.294	144	551	102	162	7	54	81	48	45
RIGHT	.252		135		34	0	11	25	10	
LEFT	.308		416		128	7	43	56	38	
Santovenia,N	.333	2	3	1	1	1	2	0	0	0
Sax,S	.236	143	567	74	134	4	47	43	42	30
Sveum,D	.219	40	114	15	25	2	12	12	29	1
RIGHT	.333		9		3	0	1	6	2	
LEFT	.210		105		22	2	11	6	27	
Thomas,F	.323	160	573	108	185	24	115	122	88	6
Ventura,R	.282	157	592	85	167	16	93	93	71	2
CHICAGO	.261	162	5498	738	1434	110	686	622	784	160
OPPONENTS	.252	162	5551	690	1400	123	658	550	810	120
DH	.238	162	668	76	159	22	104	38	108	7

CHICAGO WHITE SOX

1992 Roster

PITCHER	R/L	W	L	ERA	G	GS	SV	BB	SO	OP. AVG
Alvarez,W	L	5	3	5.20	34	9	1	65	66	.272
Drahman,B	R	0	0	2.57	5	0	0	2	1	.222
Dunne,M	R	2	0	4.26	4	1	0	6	6	.255
Fernandez,A	R	8	11	4.27	29	29	0	50	95	.270
+Hernandez,R	R	7	3	1.65	43	0	12	20	68	.180
Hibbard,G	L	10	7	4.40	31	28	1	57	69	.277
Hough,C	R	7	12	3.93	27	27	0	66	76	.239
Leach,T	R	6	5	1.95	51	0	0	20	22	.215
McCaskill,K	R	12	13	4.18	34	34	0	95	109	.242
McDowell,J	R	20	10	3.18	34	34	0	75	178	.251
Pall,D	R	5	2	4.93	39	0	1	27	27	.272
Radinsky,S	L	3	7	2.73	68	0	15	34	48	.243
Thigpen,B	R	1	3	4.75	55	0	22	33	45	.275
CHICAGO		86	76	3.82	162	162	52	550	810	.252
OPPONENTS		76	86	4.20	162	162	42	622	784	.261

Key: +Rookie *Player on the disabled list at the end of the season

CONTACT & TICKET INFORMATION

Stadium: Comiskey Park
Capacity: 44,177
Comiskey Park
333 West 35th Street
Chicago, IL 60616
General tel. number, tickets: (312) 924-1000
1993 Ticket Prices
 Club: $18
 Box: $12–15
 Reserved: $8–11
 Bleachers: $8

CLEVELAND INDIANS

Club Records (since 1900)

Batting

Batting	Joe Jackson	.408
Hitting streak	Bill Bradley	29
Home runs	Al Rosen	43
RBI	Hal Trosky	162
Hits	Joe Jackson	233
Runs	Earl Averill	140
Doubles	George Burns	64
Triples	Joe Jackson	26
Stolen bases	Miguel Dilone	61
Bases on balls	Mike Hargrove	111
Strikeouts (most)	Cory Synder	166

Pitching

Games (appearances)	Sid Monge	76
Complete games	Bob Feller	36
Innings pitched	Bob Feller	371
Games won	Jim Bagby, Sr.	31
Games lost	Pete Dowling, Luis Tiant	20
Games started	George Uhle	44
Games finished	Doug Jones	64
Bases on balls	Bob Feller	208
Strikeouts	Bob Feller	348
Saves	Doug Jones	43

CLEVELAND INDIANS

1992 Roster

PLAYER	AVG	G	AB	R	H	HR	RBI	BB	SO	SB
Alomar,S	.251	89	299	22	75	2	26	13	32	3
Baerga,C	.312	161	657	92	205	20	105	35	76	10
RIGHT	.380		166		63	4	35	3	19	
LEFT	.289		491		142	16	70	32	57	
Belle,A	.260	153	585	81	152	34	112	52	128	8
Cole,A	.206	41	97	11	20	0	5	10	21	9
Fermin,F	.270	79	215	27	58	0	13	18	10	0
+Hernandez,J	.000	3	4	0	0	0	0	0	2	0
Hill,G	.241	102	369	38	89	18	49	20	73	9
Howard,T	.277	117	358	36	99	2	32	17	60	15
RIGHT	.288		104		30	2	11	6	21	
LEFT	.272		254		69	0	21	11	39	
Jacoby,B	.261	120	291	30	76	4	36	28	54	0
+Jefferson,R	.337	24	89	8	30	1	6	1	17	0
RIGHT	.263		19		5	1	3	1	7	
LEFT	.357		70		25	0	3	0	10	
+Kirby,W	.167	21	18	9	3	1	1	3	2	0
+Levis,J	.279	28	43	2	12	1	3	0	5	0
Lewis,M	.264	122	413	44	109	5	30	25	69	4
+Lofton,K	.285	148	576	96	164	5	42	68	54	66
Martinez,C	.263	69	228	23	60	5	35	7	21	1
Ortiz,J	.250	86	244	20	61	0	24	12	23	1
Perezchica,T	.100	18	20	2	2	0	1	2	6	0
Rohde,D	.000	5	7	0	0	0	0	2	3	0
RIGHT	.000		3		0	0	0	0	3	
LEFT	.000		4		0	0	0	2	0	
Sorrento,P	.269	140	458	52	123	18	60	51	89	0
+Thome,J	.205	40	117	8	24	2	12	10	34	2
Whiten,M	.254	148	508	73	129	9	43	72	102	16
RIGHT	.283		127		36	3	8	23	21	
LEFT	.244		381		93	6	35	49	81	
Worthington,C	.167	9	24	0	4	0	2	2	4	0
CLEVELAND	.266	162	5620	674	1495	127	637	448	885	144
OPPONENTS	.268	162	5615	746	1507	159	702	566	890	109
DH	.241	162	632	78	152	27	93	52	147	7

CLEVELAND INDIANS

1992 Roster

PITCHER	R/L	W	L	ERA	G	GS	SV	BB	SO	OP.AVG
Armstrong,J	R	6	15	4.64	35	23	0	67	114	.269
Arnsberg,B	R	0	0	11.81	8	0	0	11	5	.317
Bell,E	L	0	2	7.63	7	1	0	9	10	.349
Boucher,D	L	2	2	6.37	8	7	0	20	17	.302
+Christophe,M	R	0	0	3.00	10	0	0	10	13	.254
Cook,D	L	5	7	3.82	32	25	0	50	96	.255
+Embree,A	L	0	2	7.00	4	4	0	8	12	.271
Lilliquist,D	L	5	3	1.75	71	0	6	18	47	.187
Mesa,J	R	7	12	4.59	28	27	0	70	62	.273
+Mlicki,D	R	0	2	4.98	4	4	0	16	16	.280
+Mutis,J	L	0	2	9.53	3	2	0	6	8	.429
Nagy,C	R	17	10	2.96	33	33	0	57	169	.260
Nichols,R	R	4	3	4.53	30	9	0	31	56	.273
Olin,S	R	8	5	2.34	72	0	29	27	47	.249
Otto,D	L	5	9	7.06	18	16	0	33	32	.333
Plunk,E	R	9	6	3.64	58	0	4	38	50	.229
Power,T	R	3	3	2.54	64	0	6	35	51	.248
Scudder,S	R	6	10	5.28	23	22	0	55	66	.303
Shaw,J	R	0	1	8.22	2	1	0	4	3	.259
Wickander,K	L	2	0	3.07	44	0	1	28	38	.260
CLEVELAND		76	86	4.11	162	162	46	566	890	.268
OPPONENTS		86	76	3.71	162	162	48	448	885	.266

Key: +Rookie *Player on the disabled list at the end of the season

Stadium: Cleveland Stadium
Capacity: 74,383
Cleveland Stadium
Boudreau Blvd.
Cleveland, OH 44114
General tel. number: (216) 861-1200
Tickets: (216) 241-5555
1993 Ticket Prices
    Box: $12
    Reserved: $9.50
    General: $6
    Sr. citizens, children: $5

CONTACT & TICKET INFORMATION

DETROIT TIGERS

Club Records (since 1900)

Batting

Batting	Ty Cobb	.420
Hitting streak	Ty Cobb	40
Home runs	Hank Greenberg	58
RBI	Hank Greenberg	183
Hits	Ty Cobb	248
Runs	Ty Cobb	147
Doubles	Hank Greenberg	63
Triples	Sam Crawford	26
Stolen bases	Ty Cobb	96
Bases on balls	Roy Cullenbine	137
Strikeouts (most)	Cecil Fielder	182

Pitching

Games (appearances)	Willie Hernandez	80
Complete games	George Mullin	42
Innings pitched	George Mullin	382
Games won	Denny McLain	31
Games lost	George Mullin	23
Games started	Mickey Lolich	45
Games finished	Willie Hernandez	68
Bases on balls	Joe Coleman	158
Strikeouts	Mickey Lolich	308
Saves	John Hiller	38

DETROIT TIGERS

1992 Roster

PLAYER	AVG	G	AB	R	H	HR	RBI	BB	SO	SB
Barnes,S	.273	95	165	27	45	3	25	10	18	3
Bergman,D	.232	87	181	17	42	1	10	20	19	1
+Brogna,R	.192	9	26	3	5	1	3	3	5	0
Carreon,M	.232	101	336	34	78	10	41	22	57	3
+Clark,P	.407	23	54	3	22	1	5	6	9	1
*Cuyler,M	.241	89	291	39	70	3	28	10	62	8
RIGHT	.291		86		25	2	8	3	11	
LEFT	.220		205		45	1	20	7	51	
Deer,R	.247	110	393	66	97	32	64	51	131	4
Fielder,C	.244	155	594	80	145	35	124	73	151	0
Fryman,T	.266	161	659	87	175	20	96	45	144	8
Gladden,D	.254	113	417	57	106	7	42	30	64	4
*+Hare,S	.115	15	26	0	3	0	5	2	4	0
Kreuter,C	.253	67	190	22	48	2	16	20	38	0
RIGHT	.182		66		12	1	7	10	12	
LEFT	.290		124		36	1	9	10	26	
+Livingston,S	.282	117	354	43	100	4	46	21	36	1
Pettis,G	.202	48	129	27	26	1	12	27	34	13
RIGHT	.316		38		12	0	6	8	10	2
LEFT	.154		91		14	1	6	19	24	1
Phillips,T	.276	159	606	114	167	10	64	114	93	12
RIGHT	.270		174		47	5	23	37	21	
LEFT	.278		432		120	5	41	77	72	
+Rowland,R	.214	6	14	2	3	0	0	3	3	0
Tettleton,M	.238	157	525	82	125	32	83	122	137	0
RIGHT	.274		135		37	8	23	22	28	
LEFT	.226		390		88	24	60	100	109	
*Trammell,A	.275	29	102	11	28	1	11	15	4	2
Whitaker,L	.278	130	453	77	126	19	71	81	46	6
DETROIT	.256	162	5515	791	1411	182	746	675	1055	66
OPPONENTS	.277	162	5546	794	1534	155	750	564	693	102
DH	.271	162	584	83	158	26	96	111	136	4

DETROIT TIGERS

1992 Roster

PITCHER	R/L	W	L	ERA	G	GS	SV	BB	SO	OP.AVG
Aldred,S	L	3	8	6.78	16	13	0	33	34	.307
+Doherty,J	R	7	4	3.88	47	11	3	25	37	.287
+Groom,B	L	0	5	5.82	12	7	1	22	15	.320
Gullickson,B	R	14	13	4.34	34	34	0	50	64	.267
+Haas,D	R	5	3	3.94	12	11	0	16	29	.276
Henneman,M	R	2	6	3.96	60	0	24	20	58	.256
+Kiely,J	R	4	2	2.13	39	0	0	28	18	.224
King,E	R	4	6	5.22	17	14	1	28	45	.285
+Knudsen,K	R	2	3	4.58	48	1	5	41	51	.264
Lancaster,L	R	3	4	6.33	41	1	0	51	35	.294
Leiter,M	R	8	5	4.18	35	14	0	43	75	.277
Munoz,M	L	1	2	3.00	65	0	2	25	23	.246
*Ritz,K	R	2	5	5.60	23	11	0	44	57	.278
Tanana,F	L	13	11	4.39	32	31	0	90	91	.267
Terrell,W	R	7	10	5.20	36	14	0	48	61	.298
DETROIT		75	87	4.60	162	162	36	564	693	.277
OPPONENTS		87	75	4.54	162	162	51	675	1055	.256

Key: +Rookie   *Player on the disabled list at the end of the season

Stadium: Tiger Stadium
Capacity: 52,416
Tiger Stadium
Detroit, MI 48216
General tel. number: (313) 962-4000
Credit card orders: (313) 963-7300
Group, corporate sales: (313) 962-2050
1993 Ticket Prices
   Box: $12.50
   Reserved: $7–10
   Bleachers: $4

KANSAS CITY ROYALS

Club Records (since 1900)

Batting

Batting	George Brett	.390
Hitting streak	George Brett	30
Home runs	Steve Balboni	36
RBI	Hal McRae	133
Hits	Willie Wilson	230
Runs	Willie Wilson	133
Doubles	Hal McRae	54
Triples	Willie Wilson	21
Stolen bases	Willie Wilson	83
Bases on balls	John Mayberry	122
Strikeouts (most)	Bo Jackson	172

Pitching

Games (appearances)	Dan Quisenberry	84
Complete games	Dennis Leonard	21
Innings pitched	Dennis Leonard	295
Games won	Bret Saberhagen	23
Games lost	Paul Splittorff	19
Games started	Dennis Leonard	40
Games finished	Dan Quisenberry	76
Bases on balls	Mark Gubicza	120
Strikeouts	Dennis Leonard	244
Saves	Dan Quisenberry	45

KANSAS CITY ROYALS

1992 Roster

PLAYER	AVG	G	AB	R	H	HR	RBI	BB	SO	SB
Brett,G	.285	152	592	55	169	7	61	35	69	8
+Conine,J	.253	28	91	10	23	0	9	8	23	0
Eisenreich,J	.269	113	353	31	95	2	28	24	36	11
*Gwynn,C	.286	34	84	10	24	1	7	3	10	0
Howard,D	.224	74	219	19	49	1	18	15	43	3
RIGHT	.208		72		15	0	2	2	15	
LEFT	.231		147		34	1	16	13	28	
Jefferies,G	.285	152	604	66	172	10	75	43	29	19
RIGHT	.257		179		46	3	12	7	11	
LEFT	.296		425		126	7	63	36	18	
Joyner,W	.269	149	572	66	154	9	66	55	50	11
+Koslofski,K	.248	55	133	20	33	3	13	12	23	2
Macfarlane,M	.234	129	402	51	94	17	48	30	89	1
Mayne,B	.225	82	213	16	48	0	18	11	26	0
McRae,B	.223	149	533	63	119	4	52	42	88	18
RIGHT	.233		163		38	3	20	10	27	
LEFT	.219		370		81	1	32	32	61	
McReynolds,K	.247	109	373	45	92	13	49	67	48	7
Melvin,B	.314	32	70	5	22	0	6	5	13	0
Miller,K	.284	106	416	57	118	4	38	31	46	16
+Pulliam,H	.200	4	5	2	1	0	0	1	3	0
+Rossy,R	.215	59	149	21	32	1	12	20	20	0
Samuel,J	.284	29	102	15	29	0	8	7	27	6
Shumpert,T	.149	36	94	6	14	1	11	3	17	2
Thurman,G	.245	88	200	25	49	0	20	9	34	9
Wilkerson,C	.250	111	296	27	74	2	29	18	47	18
RIGHT	.294		68		20	1	7	6	10	
LEFT	.237		228		54	1	22	12	37	
KANSAS CITY	.256	162	5501	610	1411	75	568	439	741	131
OPPONENTS	.259	162	5502	667	1426	106	628	512	834	107
DH	.278	162	643	72	179	11	62	40	88	11

KANSAS CITY ROYALS

1992 Roster

PITCHER	R/L	W	L	ERA	G	GS	SV	BB	SO	OP. AVG
Appier,K	R	15	8	2.46	30	30	0	68	150	.217
Aquino,L	R	3	6	4.52	15	13	0	20	11	.303
Berenguer,J	R	1	4	5.64	19	2	0	20	26	.247
*Boddicker,M	R	1	4	4.98	29	8	3	37	47	.270
Davis,M	L	1	3	7.18	13	6	0	28	19	.294
Gordon,T	R	6	10	4.59	40	11	0	55	98	.258
*Gubicza,M	R	7	6	3.72	18	18	0	36	81	.259
Haney,C	L	2	3	3.86	7	7	0	16	27	.226
Heaton,N	L	3	1	4.07	32	0	0	23	31	.269
+Johnston,J	R	0	0	13.50	5	0	0	2	0	.273
Magnante,M	L	4	9	4.94	44	12	0	35	31	.325
+Meacham,R	R	10	4	2.74	64	0	2	21	64	.233
+Moeller,D	R	0	3	7.00	5	4	0	11	6	.333
Montgomery,J	R	1	6	2.18	65	0	39	27	69	.205
+Pichardo,H	R	9	6	3.95	31	24	0	49	59	.267
+Pierce,E	L	0	0	3.38	2	1	0	4	3	.429
Rasmussen,D	L	4	1	1.43	5	5	0	6	12	.197
Reed,R	R	3	7	3.68	19	18	0	20	49	.271
Sampen,B	R	0	2	3.66	8	1	0	3	14	.292
+Sauveur,R	L	0	1	4.40	8	0	0	8	7	.273
+Shifflett,S	R	1	4	2.60	34	0	0	17	25	.279
Young,C	L	4	2	3.99	23	7	0	17	20	.296
KANSAS CITY		72	90	3.81	162	162	44	512	834	.259
OPPONENTS		90	72	3.39	162	162	39	439	741	.256

Stadium: Royals Stadium
Capacity: 40,625
Box 419969
Kansas City, MO 64141
General tel. number, tickets, group sales: (816) 921-2200
Credit card orders, group, corporate sales: (816) 921-4400
1993 Ticket Prices
>Box: $9–13
>Reserved: $8–10
>Royal nights: $4

CONTACT & TICKET INFORMATION

MILWAUKEE BREWERS

Club Records (since 1900)

Batting

Batting	Paul Molitor	.353
Hitting streak	Paul Molitor	39
Home runs	Gorman Thomas	45
RBI	Cecil Cooper	126
Hits	Cecil Cooper	219
Runs	Paul Molitor	136
Doubles	Robin Yount	49
Triples	Paul Molitor	16
Stolen bases	Paul Molitor	45
Bases on balls	Gorman Thomas	98
Strikeouts (most)	Rob Deer	186

Pitching

Games (appearances)	Ken Sanders	83
Complete games	Mike Caldwell	23
Innings pitched	Jim Colborn	314
Games won	Mike Caldwell	22
Games lost	Clyde Wright	20
Games started	Jim Slaton	38
Games finished	Ken Sanders	77
Bases on balls	Pete Broberg	106
Strikeouts	Ted Higuera	240
Saves	Dan Plesac	33

MILWAUKEE BREWERS

1992 Roster

PLAYER	AVG	G	AB	R	H	HR	RBI	BB	SO	SB
Allanson,A	.320	9	25	6	8	0	0	1	2	3
Bichette,D	.287	112	387	37	111	5	41	16	74	18
+Diaz,A	.111	22	9	5	1	0	1	0	0	3
RIGHT	.000		1		0	0	0	0	0	
LEFT	.125		8		1	0	1	0	0	
Fletcher,S	.275	123	386	53	106	3	51	30	33	17
Gantner,J	.246	101	256	22	63	1	18	12	17	6
Hamilton,D	.298	128	470	67	140	5	62	45	42	41
+Jaha,J	.226	47	133	17	30	2	10	12	30	10
+Listach,P	.290	149	579	93	168	1	47	55	124	54
RIGHT	.345		148		51	1	18	8	25	
LEFT	.271		431		117	0	29	47	99	
+McIntosh,T	.182	35	77	7	14	0	6	3	9	1
Molitor,P	.320	158	609	89	195	12	89	73	66	31
+Nilsson,D	.232	51	164	15	38	4	25	17	18	2
Seitzer,K	.270	148	540	74	146	5	71	57	44	13
Spiers,B	.313	12	16	2	5	0	2	1	4	1
Stubbs,F	.229	92	288	37	66	9	42	27	68	11
+Suero,W	.188	18	16	4	3	0	0	2	1	1
Surhoff,B	.252	139	480	63	121	4	62	46	41	14
+Tatum,J	.125	5	8	0	1	0	0	1	2	0
+Valentin,J	.000	4	3	1	0	0	1	0	0	0
RIGHT	.000		0		0	0	0	0	0	
LEFT	.000		3		0	0	1	0	0	
Vaughn,G	.228	141	501	77	114	23	78	60	123	15
Yount,R	.264	150	557	71	147	8	77	53	81	15
MILWAUKEE	.268	162	5504	740	1477	82	683	511	779	256
OPPONENTS	.246	162	5468	604	1344	127	576	435	793	95
DH	.290	162	621	76	180	12	88	79	88	34

MILWAUKEE BREWERS

1992 Roster

PITCHER	R/L	W	L	ERA	G	GS	SV	BB	SO	OP.AVG
+Austin,J	R	5	2	1.85	47	0	0	32	30	.191
Bones,R	R	9	10	4.57	31	28	0	48	65	.264
Bosio,C	R	16	6	3.62	33	33	0	44	120	.254
+Eldred,C	R	11	2	1.79	14	14	0	23	62	.207
Fetters,M	R	5	1	1.87	50	0	2	24	43	.185
Heaton,N	L	3	1	4.07	32	0	0	23	31	.269
Henry,D	R	1	4	4.02	68	0	29	24	52	.256
Holmes,D	R	4	4	2.55	41	0	6	11	31	.224
Navarro,J	R	17	11	3.33	34	34	0	64	100	.246
Nunez,E	R	1	3	4.85	49	0	3	22	49	.268
Orosco,J	L	3	1	3.23	59	0	1	40	40	.232
Plesac,D	L	5	4	2.96	44	4	1	35	54	.229
*Robinson,R	R	1	4	5.86	8	8	0	14	12	.331
Ruffin,B	L	1	6	6.67	25	6	0	41	45	.293
Wegman,B	R	13	14	3.20	35	35	0	55	127	.250
MILWAUKEE		92	70	3.43	162	162	39	435	793	.246
OPPONENTS		70	92	4.03	162	162	36	511	779	.268

Key: +Rookie   *Player on the disabled list at the end of the season

CONTACT & TICKET INFORMATION

Stadium: County Stadium
Capacity: 53,192
Box 3099
Milwaukee, MI 53201
General tel. number: (414) 933-4114
Tickets: (414) 933-1818
Credit card orders: (414) 933-9000
Group, corporate sales: (414) 933-1818
1993 Ticket Prices
  Deluxe mezzanine and mezzanine: $15
  Box: $12–14
  Grandstand: $8–11
  General: $7
  Bleachers: $4

MINNESOTA TWINS

Club Records (since 1900)

Batting

Batting	Rod Carew	.388
Hitting streak	Ken Landreaux	31
Home runs	Harmon Killebrew	49
RBI	Harmon Killebrew	140
Hits	Rod Carew	239
Runs	Rod Carew	128
Doubles	Zoilo Versailles, Kirby Puckett	45
Triples	Rod Carew	16
Stolen bases	Rod Carew	49
Bases on balls	Harmon Killebrew	145
Strikeouts (most)	Bobby Darwin	145

Pitching

Games (appearances)	Mike Marshall	90
Complete games	Bert Blyleven	25
Innings pitched	Bert Blyleven	325
Games won	Jim Kaat	25
Games lost	Pedro Ramos	20
Games started	Jim Kaat	42
Games finished	Mike Marhsall	84
Bases on balls	Jim Hughes	127
Strikeouts	Bert Blyleven	258
Saves	Jeff Reardon, Rick Aguilera	42

MINNESOTA TWINS

1992 Roster

PLAYER	AVG	G	AB	R	H	HR	RBI	BB	SO	SB
+Brito,B	.143	8	14	1	2	0	2	0	4	0
+Brown,J	.067	35	15	8	1	0	0	2	4	2
+Bruett,J	.250	56	76	7	19	0	2	6	12	6
Bush,R	.214	100	182	14	39	2	22	11	37	1
Davis,C	.288	138	444	63	128	12	66	73	76	4
RIGHT	.256		121		31	4	22	13	25	
LEFT	.300		323		97	8	44	60	51	
Gagne,G	.246	146	439	53	108	7	39	19	83	6
Harper,B	.307	140	502	58	154	9	73	26	22	0
Hill,D	.294	25	51	7	15	0	2	5	6	0
RIGHT	.000		2		0	0	0	0	1	
LEFT	.306		49		15	0	2	5	5	
*Hrbek,K	.244	112	394	52	96	15	58	71	56	5
+Jorgensen,T	.310	22	58	5	18	0	5	3	11	1
Knoblauch,C	.297	155	600	104	178	2	56	88	60	34
Larkin,G	.246	115	337	38	83	6	42	28	43	7
RIGHT	.218		55		12	0	5	6	8	
LEFT	.252		282		71	6	37	22	35	
Leius,S	.249	129	409	50	102	2	35	34	61	6
Mack,S	.315	156	600	101	189	16	75	64	106	26
Munoz,P	.270	127	418	44	113	12	71	17	90	4
Pagliarulo,M	.200	42	105	10	21	0	9	1	17	1
+Parks,D	.333	7	6	1	2	0	0	1	1	0
Puckett,K	.329	160	639	104	210	19	110	44	97	17
Quinones,L	.200	3	5	0	1	0	1	0	0	0
RIGHT	.000		0		0	0	0	0	0	
LEFT	.200		5		1	0	1	0	0	
+Reboulet,J	.190	73	137	15	26	1	16	23	26	3
+Reed,D	.182	14	33	2	6	0	4	2	11	0
+Webster,L	.280	53	118	10	33	1	13	9	11	0
MINNESOTA	.277	162	5582	747	1544	104	701	527	834	123
OPPONENTS	.254	162	5472	653	1391	121	618	479	923	152
DH	.271	162	591	82	160	12	80	91	104	11

48

MINNESOTA TWINS

1992 Roster

PITCHER	R/L	W	L	ERA	G	GS	SV	BB	SO	OP. AVG
Abbott,P	R	0	0	3.27	6	0	0	5	13	.279
Aguilera,R	R	2	6	2.84	64	0	41	17	52	.238
+Banks,W	R	4	4	5.70	16	12	0	37	37	.288
Casian,L	L	1	0	2.70	6	0	0	1	2	.259
Edens,T	R	6	3	2.83	52	0	3	36	57	.236
Erickson,S	R	13	12	3.40	32	32	0	83	101	.252
+Gozzo,M	R	0	0	27.00	2	0	0	0	1	.583
Guthrie,M	L	2	3	2.88	54	0	5	23	76	.215
Kipper,B	L	3	3	4.42	25	0	0	14	22	.268
Krueger,B	L	10	6	4.30	27	27	0	46	86	.263
+Mahomes,P	R	3	4	5.04	14	13	0	37	44	.279
Smiley,J	L	16	9	3.21	34	34	0	65	163	.231
Tapani,K	R	16	11	3.97	34	34	0	48	138	.269
+Trombley,M	R	3	2	3.30	10	7	0	17	38	.247
Wayne,G	L	3	3	2.63	41	0	0	19	29	.260
West,D	L	1	3	6.99	9	3	0	20	19	.276
Willis,C	R	7	3	2.72	59	0	1	11	45	.246
MINNESOTA		90	72	3.70	162	162	50	479	923	.254
OPPONENTS		72	90	4.17	162	162	38	527	834	.277

Key: +Rookie   *Player on the disabled list at the end of the season

Stadium: Hubert H. Humphrey Metrodome
Capacity: 55,883
Metrodome
501 S. Chicago Ave., So.
Minneapolis, MN 55415
General tel. number: (612) 375-1366
Tickets: (612) 375-1116 or (800) 28T-WINS
Group, corporate sales: (612) 375-7454
1993 Ticket Prices
   Club: $11–14
   Reserved: $10–12
   Low leftfield: $7
   General: $4

CONTACT & TICKET INFORMATION

NEW YORK YANKEES

Club Records (since 1900)

Batting		
Batting	Babe Ruth	.393
Hitting streak	Joe DiMaggio	56
Home runs	Roger Maris	61
RBI	Lou Gehrig	184
Hits	Don Mattingly	238
Runs	Babe Ruth	177
Doubles	Don Mattingly	53
Triples	Earle Combs	23
Stolen bases	Rickey Henderson	93
Bases on balls	Babe Ruth	170
Strikeouts (most)	Jesse Barfield	150

Pitching		
Games (appearances)	Dave Righetti	74
Complete games	Jack Chesbro	48
Innings pitched	Jack Chesbro	454
Games won	Jack Chesbro	41
Games lost	Al Orth, Joe Lake, Russel Ford, Sam Jones	21
Games started	Jack Chesbro	51
Games finished	Dave Righetti	68
Bases on balls	Tommy Byrne	179
Strikeouts	Ron Guidry	248
Saves	Dave Righetti	46

NEW YORK YANKEES

1992 Roster

PLAYER	AVG	G	AB	R	H	HR	RBI	BB	SO	SB
* Barfield,J	.137	30	95	8	13	2	7	9	27	1
Gallego,M	.254	53	173	24	44	3	14	20	22	0
Hall,M	.280	152	583	67	163	15	81	29	53	4
Hayes,C	.257	142	509	52	131	18	66	28	100	3
+Humphreys,M	.100	4	10	0	1	0	0	0	1	0
James,D	.262	67	145	24	38	3	17	22	15	1
Kelly,P	.226	106	318	38	72	7	27	25	72	8
Kelly,R	.272	152	580	81	158	10	66	41	96	28
Leyritz,J	.257	63	144	17	37	7	26	14	22	0
Maas,K	.248	98	286	35	71	11	35	25	63	3
Mattingly,D	.288	157	640	89	184	14	86	39	43	3
Meulens,H	.600	2	5	1	3	1	1	1	0	0
Nokes,M	.224	121	384	42	86	22	59	37	62	0
+Silvestri,D	.308	7	13	3	4	0	1	0	3	0
+Snow,J	.143	7	14	1	2	0	2	5	5	0
RIGHT	.000		3		0	0	0	0	1	
LEFT	.182		11		2	0	2	5	4	
+Stankiewic,A	.268	116	400	52	107	2	25	38	42	9
Stanley,M	.249	68	173	24	43	8	27	33	45	0
Tartabull,D	.266	123	421	72	112	25	85	14	2	2
Velarde,R	.272	121	412	57	112	7	46	38	78	7
Williams,B	.280	62	261	39	73	5	26	29	36	7
RIGHT	.298		84		25	1	9	10	11	
LEFT	.271		177		48	4	17	19	25	
+Williams,G	.296	15	27	7	8	3	6	0	3	2
NEW YORK	.261	162	5593	733	1462	163	703	536	903	78
OPPONENTS	.263	162	5517	746	1453	129	700	612	851	164
DH	.245	162	613	81	150	22	90	75	126	2

NEW YORK YANKEES

1992 Roster

PITCHER	R/L	W	L	ERA	G	GS	SV	BB	SO	OP. AVG
Burke,T	R	2	2	3.25	23	0	0	15	8	.250
Cadaret,G	L	4	8	4.25	46	11	1	74	73	.267
Farr,S	R	2	2	1.56	50	0	30	19	37	.186
Guetterman,L	L	1	1	9.53	15	0	0	13	5	.354
Habyan,J	R	5	6	3.84	56	0	7	21	44	.295
Hillegas,S	R	1	8	5.23	26	9	0	37	49	.303
+Hitchcock,S	L	0	2	8.31	3	3	0	6	6	.377
Howe,S	L	3	0	2.45	20	0	6	3	12	.122
Johnson,J	R	2	3	6.66	13	8	0	23	14	.329
Kamienieck,S	R	6	14	4.36	28	28	0	74	88	.269
Leary,T	R	8	10	5.36	26	23	0	87	46	.256
+Militello,S	R	3	3	3.45	9	9	0	32	42	.195
Monteleone,R	R	7	3	3.30	47	0	0	27	62	.235
+Nielsen,G	L	1	0	4.58	20	0	0	18	12	.243
Perez,M	R	13	16	2.87	33	33	0	93	218	.235
Sanderson,S	R	12	11	4.93	33	33	0	64	104	.286
+Springer,R	R	0	0	6.19	14	0	0	10	12	.281
+Wickman,B	R	6	1	4.11	8	8	0	20	21	.273
Young,C	L	4	2	3.99	23	7	0	17	20	.296
NEW YORK		76	86	4.21	162	162	44	612	851	.263
OPPONENTS		86	76	4.21	162	162	53	536	903	.261

Key: +Rookie   *Player on the disabled list at the end of the season

CONTACT & TICKET INFORMATION

Stadium: Yankee Stadium
Capacity: 57,545
Yankee Stadium
Bronx, NY 10451
General tel. number: (718) 293-4300
Credit card orders: (718) 293-6000
Group, corporate sales, season tickets: (718) 293-6013
1993 Ticket Prices
  Box: $14.50–16
  Reserved: $10.50–13.50
  General: $6.50
  Sr. citizens: $1

OAKLAND ATHLETICS

Club Records (since 1900)

Batting

Batting	Carney Lansford	.336
Hitting streak	Carney Lansford	24
Home runs	Mark McGwire	49
RBI	Jose Canseco	124
Hits	Jose Canseco	187
Runs	Reggie Jackson	123
Doubles	Joe Rudi, Reggie Jackson	39
Triples	Phil Garner	12
Stolen bases	Rickey Henderson	130
Bases on balls	Sal Bando	118
Strikeouts (most)	Jose Canseco	175

Pitching

Games (appearances)	Rollie Fingers	76
Complete games	Rick Langford	28
Innings pitched	Jim Hunter	318
Games won	Bob Welch	27
Games lost	Brain Kingman	20
Games started	Jim Hunter	41
Games finished	Rollie Fingers, Bill Caudill	62
Bases on balls	John Odom	112
Strikeouts	Vida Blue	301
Saves	Dennis Eckersley	48

OAKLAND ATHLETICS

1992 Roster

PLAYER	AVG	G	AB	R	H	HR	RBI	BB	SO	SB
Baines,H	.253	140	478	58	121	16	76	59	61	1
Blankenshi,L	.241	123	349	59	84	3	34	82	57	21
Bordick,M	.300	154	504	62	151	3	48	40	59	12
+Brosius,S	.218	38	87	13	19	4	13	3	13	3
Browne,J	.287	111	324	43	93	3	40	40	40	3
RIGHT	.184		49		9	0	5	3	6	
LEFT	.305		275		84	3	35	37	34	
Canseco,J	.244	119	439	74	107	26	87	63	128	6
+Fox,E	.238	51	143	24	34	3	13	13	29	3
RIGHT	.227		22		5	0	1	2	6	
LEFT	.240		121		29	3	12	11	23	
Hemond,S	.225	25	40	8	9	0	2	4	13	1
Henderson,D	.143	20	63	1	9	0	2	2	16	0
Henderson,R	.283	117	396	77	112	15	46	95	56	48
+Howitt,D	.188	35	85	7	16	2	10	8	9	1
Kingery,M	.107	12	28	3	3	0	1	1	3	0
Lansford,C	.262	135	496	65	130	7	75	43	39	7
McGwire,M	.268	139	467	87	125	42	104	90	105	0
+Mercedes,H	.800	9	5	1	4	0	1	0	1	0
+Neel,T	.264	24	53	8	14	3	9	5	15	0
Nelson,G	.000	29	0	1	0	0	0	0	0	0
Quirk,J	.220	78	177	13	39	2	11	16	28	0
Ready,R	.200	61	125	17	25	3	17	25	23	1
Sierra,R	.278	151	601	83	167	17	87	45	68	14
RIGHT	.346		26		9	2	8	4	1	
LEFT	.253		75		19	1	9	10	8	
Steinbach,T	.279	128	438	48	122	12	53	45	58	2
Weiss,W	.212	103	316	36	67	0	21	43	39	6
RIGHT	.135		74		10	0	2	5	3	
LEFT	.236		242		57	0	19	38	36	
Wilson,W	.270	132	396	38	107	0	37	35	65	28
RIGHT	.248		121		30	0	14	13	30	
LEFT	.280		275		77	0	23	22	35	
OAKLAND	.258	162	5387	745	1389	142	693	707	831	143
OPPONENTS	.256	162	5446	672	1396	129	630	601	843	118
DH	.244	162	622	88	152	26	108	80	107	5

OAKLAND ATHLETICS

1992 Roster

PITCHER	R/L	W	L	ERA	G	GS	SV	BB	SO	OP.AVG
+Briscoe,J	R	0	1	6.43	2	2	0	9	4	.400
+Campbell,K	R	2	3	5.12	32	5	1	45	38	.267
Corsi,J	R	4	2	1.43	32	0	0	18	19	.275
Darling,R	R	15	10	3.66	33	33	0	72	99	.253
Downs,K	R	5	5	3.29	18	13	0	46	38	.237
Eckersley,D	R	7	1	1.91	69	0	51	11	93	.211
Gossage,R	R	0	2	2.84	30	0	0	19	26	.230
+Guzman,J	L	0	0	12.00	2	0	0	0	0	.471
Hillegas,S	R	1	8	5.23	26	9	0	37	49	.303
Honeycutt,R	L	1	4	3.69	54	0	3	10	32	.272
+Horsman,V	L	2	1	2.49	58	0	1	21	18	.252
Moore,M	R	17	12	4.12	36	36	0	103	117	.269
Nelson,G	R	3	1	6.45	28	2	0	22	23	.335
Parrett,J	R	9	1	3.02	66	0	0	42	78	.226
+Raczka,M	L	0	0	8.53	8	0	0	5	2	.308
+Revenig,T	R	0	0	0.00	2	0	0	0	1	.286
Russell,J	R	4	3	1.63	59	0	30	25	48	.224
Slusarski,J	R	5	5	5.45	15	14	0	27	38	.284
Stewart,D	R	12	10	3.66	31	31	0	79	130	.237
+Walton,B	R	0	0	9.90	7	0	0	3	7	.378
Welch,B	R	11	7	3.27	20	20	0	43	47	.247
Witt,B	R	10	14	4.29	31	31	0	114	125	.256
OAKLAND		96	66	3.73	162	162	58	601	843	.256
OPPONENTS		66	96	4.23	162	162	38	707	831	.258

Key: +Rookie *Player on the disabled list at the end of the season

Stadium: Oakland Alameda Co. Coliseum
Capacity: 47,313
Oakland Coliseum
Oakland, CA 94621
General tel. number: (510) 638-4900
Tickets: (510) 568-5600
1993 Ticket Prices
- MVP: $14
- Field: $13–14
- Plaza: $11–13
- Upper reserved: $7
- Bleachers: $4.50

CONTACT & TICKET INFORMATION

SEATTLE MARINERS

Club Records (since 1900)

Batting

Batting	Ken Griffey, Jr.	.327
Hitting streak	Dan Meyer, Richie Zisk	21
Home runs	Gorman Thomas	32
RBI	Alvin Davis	116
Hits	Phil Bradley	192
Runs	Ruppert Jones	109
Doubles	Ken Griffey, Jr.	42
Triples	Harold Reynolds	11
Stolen bases	Harold Reynolds	60
Bases on balls	Alvin Davis	101
Strikeouts (most)	Jim Presley	172

Pitching

Games (appearances)	Ed Vande Berg	78
Complete games	Mike Moore, Mark Langston	14
Innings pitched	Mark Langston	272
Games won	Mark Langston	19
Games lost	Matt Young, Mike Moore	19
Games started	Mike Moore	37
Games finished	Bill Caudill	64
Bases on balls	Randy Johnson	152
Strikeouts	Mark Langston	262
Saves	Mike Schooler	33

SEATTLE MARINERS

1992 Roster

PLAYER	AVG	G	AB	R	H	HR	RBI	BB	SO	SB
+Amaral,R	.240	35	100	9	24	1	7	5	16	4
Blowers,M	.192	31	73	7	14	1	2	6	20	0
+Boone,B	.194	33	129	15	25	4	15	4	34	1
Bradley,S	.000	2	1	0	0	0	0	1	1	0
Briley,G	.275	86	200	18	55	5	12	4	31	9
Buhner,J	.243	152	543	69	132	25	79	71	146	0
*Cochrane,D	.250	65	152	10	38	2	12	12	34	1
RIGHT	.276		58		16	1	3	5	15	
LEFT	.234		94		22	1	9	7	19	
Cotto,H	.259	108	294	42	76	5	27	14	49	23
Griffey Jr,K	.308	142	565	83	174	27	103	44	67	10
+Haselman,B	.263	8	19	1	5	0	0	0	7	0
+Heffernan,B	.091	8	11	0	1	0	1	0	1	0
+Howitt,D	.188	35	85	7	16	2	10	8	9	1
+Lennon,P	.000	1	2	0	0	0	0	0	0	0
Martinez,E	.343	135	528	100	181	18	73	54	61	14
Martinez,T	.257	136	460	53	118	16	66	42	77	2
*Mitchell,K	.286	99	360	48	103	9	67	35	46	0
Moses,J	.136	21	22	3	3	0	1	5	4	0
RIGHT	.000		3		0	0	0	0	0	
LEFT	.158		19		3	0	1	5	4	
O'Brien,P	.222	134	396	40	88	14	52	40	27	2
Parrish,L	.233	93	275	26	64	12	32	24	70	1
Reynolds,H	.247	140	458	55	113	3	33	45	41	15
RIGHT	.250		116		29	0	12	17	4	
LEFT	.246		342		84	3	21	28	37	
Schaefer,J	.114	65	70	5	8	1	3	2	10	0
*Sinatro,M	.107	18	28	0	3	0	0	0	5	0
+Turner,S	.270	34	74	8	20	0	5	9	15	2
Valle,D	.240	124	367	39	88	9	30	27	58	0
Vizquel,O	.294	136	483	49	142	0	21	32	38	15
RIGHT	.229		105		24	0	5	8	4	
LEFT	.312		378		118	0	16	24	34	
SEATTLE	.263	162	5564	679	1466	149	638	474	841	100
OPPONENTS	.266	162	5519	799	1467	129	755	661	894	140
DH	.275	162	625	84	172	22	88	56	87	10

SEATTLE MARINERS

1992 Roster

PITCHER	R/L	W	L	ERA	G	GS	SV	BB	SO	OP. AVG
Acker,J	R	0	0	5.28	17	0	0	12	11	.338
Agosto,J	L	0	0	5.89	17	1	0	3	12	.346
+Barton,S	L	0	1	2.92	14	0	0	7	4	.238
Brown,K	L	0	0	9.00	2	0	0	3	2	.333
Delucia,R	R	3	6	5.49	30	11	1	35	66	.293
Fisher,B	R	4	3	4.53	22	14	1	47	26	.234
+Fleming,D	L	17	10	3.39	33	33	0	60	112	.257
Grant,M	R	2	4	3.89	23	10	0	22	42	.311
+Gunderson,E	L	2	1	8.68	9	0	0	5	2	.324
Hanson,E	R	8	17	4.82	31	30	0	57	112	.287
Harris,G	R	0	0	7.00	8	0	0	6	6	.235
Johnson,R	L	12	14	3.77	31	31	0	144	241	.206
Jones,C	R	3	5	5.69	38	1	0	47	49	.226
Kramer,R	R	0	1	7.71	4	4	0	7	6	.400
Leary,T	R	8	10	5.36	26	23	0	87	46	.256
+Nelson,J	R	1	7	3.44	66	0	6	44	46	.245
*Parker,C	R	0	2	7.56	8	6	0	11	20	.338
Powell,D	L	4	2	4.58	49	0	0	29	35	.238
Schmidt,D	R	0	0	18.90	3	0	0	3	1	.438
Schooler,M	R	2	7	4.70	53	0	13	24	33	.275
Swan,R	L	3	10	4.74	55	9	9	45	45	.262
+Walker,M	R	0	3	7.36	5	3	0	9	5	.333
*+Woodson,K	R	0	1	3.29	8	1	0	11	6	.245
SEATTLE		64	98	4.55	162	162	30	661	894	.266
OPPONENTS		98	64	3.84	162	162	57	474	841	.263

Key: +Rookie *Player on the disabled list at the end of the season

CONTACT & TICKET INFORMATION

Stadium: The Kingdome
Capacity: 59,702
Box 4100
Seattle, WA 98104
General tel. number, tickets: (206) 628-3555
Credit card orders: (206) 628-0888
1993 Ticket Prices
  Box: $11.50
  Field: $10.50
  Club: $8.50
  View: $3.50–5.50
  Family: $2.50–4.50
  General: $2.50

TEXAS RANGERS

Club Records (since 1900)

Batting		
Batting	Julio Franco	.341
Hitting streak	Mickey Rivers	24
Home runs	Larry Parrish	32
RBI	Ruben Sierra	119
Hits	Mickey Rivers	210
Runs	Rafael Palmeiro	115
Doubles	Rafael Palmeiro	49
Triples	Ruben Sierra	14
Stolen bases	Bump Wills	52
Bases on balls	Toby Harrah	113
Strikeouts (most)	Pete Incaviglia	185

Pitching		
Games (appearances)	Mitch Williams	85
Complete games	Ferguson Jenkins	29
Innings pitched	Ferguson Jenkins	328
Games won	Ferguson Jenkins	25
Games lost	Jim Bibby	19
Games started	Jim Bibby, Ferguson Jenkins	41
Games finished	Jeff Russell	66
Bases on balls	Bobby Witt	143
Strikeouts	Nolan Ryan	301
Saves	Jeff Russell	38

TEXAS RANGERS

1992 Roster

PLAYER	AVG	G	AB	R	H	HR	RBI	BB	SO	SB
Cangelosi,J	.188	73	85	12	16	1	6	18	16	6
RIGHT	.158		19		3	1	3	7	3	
LEFT	.197		66		13	0	3	11	13	
Canseco,J	.244	119	439	74	107	26	87	63	128	6
+Colon,C	.167	14	36	5	6	0	1	1	8	0
RIGHT	.200		15		3	0	1	1	3	
LEFT	.143		21		3	0	0	0	5	
Daugherty,J	.205	59	127	13	26	0	9	16	21	2
RIGHT	.167		30		5	0	1	2	6	
LEFT	.216		97		21	0	8	14	15	
+Davis,D	1.000	1	1	0	1	0	0	0	0	0
Diaz,M	.226	19	31	2	7	0	1	1	2	0
Downing,B	.278	107	320	53	89	10	39	62	58	1
+Fariss,M	.217	67	166	13	36	3	21	17	51	0
*Franco,J	.234	35	107	19	25	2	8	15	17	1
Frye,J	.256	67	199	24	51	1	12	16	27	1
Gonzalez,J	.260	155	584	77	152	43	109	35	143	0
+Harris,D	.182	24	33	3	6	0	1	0	15	1
+Hulse,D	.304	32	92	14	28	0	2	3	18	3
Huson,J	.261	123	318	49	83	4	24	41	43	18
+Maurer,R	.222	8	9	1	2	0	1	1	2	0
+McGinnis,R	.242	14	33	2	8	0	4	3	7	0
Newman,A	.220	116	246	25	54	0	12	34	26	9
RIGHT	.268		56		15	0	3	14	9	
LEFT	.205		190		39	0	9	20	17	
Palmeiro,R	.268	159	608	84	163	22	85	72	83	2
Palmer,D	.229	152	541	74	124	26	72	62	154	10
+Peltier,D	.167	12	24	1	4	0	2	0	3	0
Petralli,G	.198	94	192	11	38	1	18	20	34	0
Reimer,K	.267	148	494	56	132	16	58	42	103	2
Rodriguez,I	.260	123	420	39	109	8	37	24	73	0
*Russell,J	.100	7	10	1	1	0	2	1	4	0
Sierra,R	.278	151	601	83	167	17	87	45	68	14
RIGHT	.338		145		49	3	25	10	12	
LEFT	.254		355		90	11	45	21	47	
+Stephens,R	.154	8	13	0	2	0	0	0	5	0
Thon,D	.247	95	275	30	68	4	37	20	40	12
OPPONENTS	.264	162	5568	753	1471	113	690	598	1034	87
DH	.252	162	614	92	155	19	70	87	119	4

TEXAS RANGERS

1992 Roster

PITCHER	R/L	W	L	ERA	G	GS	SV	BB	SO	OP.AVG
Alexander,G	R	1	0	27.00	3	0	0	1	1	.500
Bannister,F	L	1	1	6.32	36	0	0	21	30	.281
Bohanon,B	L	1	1	6.31	18	7	0	25	29	.297
Brown,K	R	21	11	3.32	35	35	0	76	173	.260
Burns,T	R	3	5	3.84	35	10	1	32	55	.249
Campbell,M	R	0	1	9.82	1	0	0	2	2	.231
Carman,D	L	0	0	7.71	2	0	0	0	2	.364
Chiamparin,S	R	0	4	3.55	4	4	0	5	13	.260
Fireovid,S	R	1	0	4.05	3	0	0	4	0	.370
Guzman,J	R	16	11	3.66	33	33	0	73	179	.268
Jeffcoat,M	L	0	1	7.32	6	3	0	5	6	.350
*+Leon,D	R	1	1	5.89	15	0	0	10	15	.254
+Manuel,B	R	1	0	4.76	3	0	0	1	9	.261
Mathews,T	R	2	4	5.95	40	0	0	31	26	.294
McCullers,L	R	1	0	5.40	5	0	0	8	3	.067
Nunez,E	R	1	3	4.85	49	0	3	22	49	.268
+Pavlik,R	R	4	4	4.21	13	12	0	34	45	.280
Robinson,J	R	4	4	5.72	16	4	0	21	18	.281
Rogers,K	L	3	6	3.09	81	0	6	26	70	.261
Rosenthal,W	R	0	0	7.71	6	0	0	2	1	.333
Russell,J	R	4	3	1.63	59	0	30	25	48	.224
Ryan,N	R	5	9	3.72	27	27	0	69	157	.238
+Smith,D	L	0	3	5.02	4	2	0	8	5	.321
+Whiteside,M	R	1	1	1.93	20	0	4	11	13	.245
Witt,B	R	10	14	4.29	31	31	0	114	125	.256
TEXAS		77	85	4.09	162	162	42	598	1034	.264
OPPONENTS		85	77	3.79	162	162	46	550	1036	.250

Key: +Rookie *Player on the disabled list at the end of the season

---

Stadium: Arlington Stadium
Capacity: 43,521
Box 90111
1250 Copeland Road
Arlington, TX 76004
General tel. number: (817) 273-5222
Tickets: (817) 273-5100

Group, corporate sales: (817) 273-5000
1993 Ticket Prices
  Box: $13–14
  Plaza: $9
  Reserved: $7
  General: $4
  Children : $2

CONTACT & TICKET INFORMATION

TORONTO BLUE JAYS

Club Records (since 1900)

Batting

Batting	Tony Fernandez	.322
Hitting streak	George Bell	22
Home runs	George Bell	47
RBI	George Bell	134
Hits	Tony Fernandez	213
Runs	George Bell	111
Doubles	Joe Carter	42
Triples	Tony Fernandez	17
Stolen bases	Dave Collins	60
Bases on balls	Fred McGriff	119
Strikeouts (most)	Fred McGriff	149

Pitching

Games (appearances)	Mark Eichhorn	89
Complete games	Dave Stieb	19
Innings pitched	Dave Stieb	288
Games won	Dave Stieb	18
Games lost	Jerry Garvin, Phil Huffman	18
Games started	Jim Clancy	40
Games finished	Tom Henke	62
Bases on balls	Jim Clancy	128
Strikeouts	Dave Stieb	198
Saves	Tom Henke	34

TORONTO BLUE JAYS

1992 Roster

PLAYER	AVG	G	AB	R	H	HR	RBI	BB	SO	SB
Alomar,R	.310	152	571	105	177	8	76	87	52	49
RIGHT	.308		156		48	5	23	25	17	
LEFT	.311		415		129	3	53	62	35	
+Bell,D	.242	61	161	23	39	2	15	15	34	7
Borders,P	.242	138	480	47	116	13	53	33	75	1
Carter,J	.264	158	622	97	164	34	119	36	109	12
Ducey,R	.188	54	80	7	15	0	2	5	22	2
Griffin,A	.233	63	150	21	35	0	10	9	19	3
RIGHT	.310		29		9	0	2	4	3	
LEFT	.215		121		26	0	8	5	16	
Gruber,K	.229	120	446	42	102	11	43	26	72	7
+Kent,J	.240	65	192	36	46	8	35	20	47	2
+Knorr,R	.263	8	19	1	5	1	2	1	5	0
Lee,M	.263	128	396	49	104	3	39	50	73	6
RIGHT	.212		118		25	0	12	15	17	
LEFT	.284		278		79	3	27	35	56	
+Maksudian,M	.000	3	3	0	0	0	0	0	0	0
Maldonado,C	.272	137	489	64	133	20	66	59	112	2
+Martinez,D	.625	7	8	2	5	1	3	0	1	0
Mulliniks,R	.500	3	2	1	1	0	0	1	0	0
*Myers,G	.231	30	78	4	18	1	13	5	11	0
Olerud,J	.284	138	458	68	130	16	66	70	61	1
+Quinlan,T	.067	13	15	2	1	0	2	2	9	0
Sprague,E	.234	22	47	6	11	1	7	3	7	0
Tabler,P	.252	49	135	11	34	0	16	11	14	0
Ward,T	.345	18	29	7	10	1	3	4	4	0
RIGHT	.625		8		5	0	2	1	0	
LEFT	.238		21		5	1	1	3	4	
White,D	.248	153	641	98	159	17	60	47	133	37
RIGHT	.212		179		38	5	19	13	41	
LEFT	.262		462		121	12	41	34	92	
Winfield,D	.290	156	583	92	169	26	108	82	89	2
+Zosky,E	.286	8	7	1	2	0	1	0	2	0
TORONTO	.263	162	5536	780	1458	163	737	561	933	129
OPPONENTS	.248	162	5432	682	1346	124	642	541	954	144
DH	.267	162	619	95	165	29	112	78	101	2

TORONTO BLUE JAYS

1992 Roster

PITCHER	R/L	W	L	ERA	G	GS	SV	BB	SO	OP. AVG
Cone,D	R	4	3	2.55	8	7	0	29	47	.207
Eichhorn,M	R	4	4	3.08	65	0	2	25	61	.255
Guzman,J	R	16	5	2.64	28	28	0	72	165	.207
Henke,T	R	3	2	2.26	57	0	34	22	46	.197
+Hentgen,P	R	5	2	5.36	28	2	0	32	39	.254
Key,J	L	13	13	3.53	33	33	0	59	117	.248
Leiter,A	L	0	0	9.00	1	0	0	2	0	.200
+Linton,D	R	1	3	8.63	8	3	0	17	16	.323
MacDonald,B	L	1	0	4.37	27	0	0	16	26	.270
Morris,J	R	21	6	4.04	34	34	0	80	132	.246
*Stieb,D	R	4	6	5.04	21	14	0	43	45	.275
Stottlemyr,T	R	12	11	4.50	28	27	0	63	98	.262
Timlin,M	R	0	2	4.12	26	0	1	20	35	.271
+Trlicek,R	R	0	0	10.80	2	0	0	2	1	.286
Ward,D	R	7	4	1.95	79	0	12	39	103	.207
+Weathers,D	R	0	0	8.10	2	0	0	2	3	.385
Wells,D	L	7	9	5.40	41	14	2	36	62	.289
TORONTO		96	66	3.91	162	162	49	541	954	.248
OPPONENTS		66	96	4.40	162	162	36	561	933	.263

Key: +Rookie *Player on the disabled list at the end of the season

CONTACT & TICKET INFORMATION

Stadium: SkyDome
Capacity: 50,516
The SkyDome
300 Bremner Blvd.
Ste. 3000
Toronto, Ont.
M5V 3B3 Canada
General tel. number: (416) 341-1000
Tickets: (416) 341-tk
1993 Ticket Prices
  Esplanade field level, Sky club level: $17.50
  Sky deck level (1st to 3rd base), Esplanade (outfield): $13.50
  Sky deck (four lines): $10
  Sky deck (outfield): $4